RubyMotion iOS Development Essentials

Create apps that utilize iOS device capabilities without learning Objective-C

Abhishek Nalwaya

Akshat Paul

PUBLISHING

BIRMINGHAM - MUMBAI

RubyMotion iOS Development Essentials

First published: July 2013

Production Reference: 1090713

Published by Packt Publishing Ltd.
Livery Place
35 Livery Street
Birmingham B3 2PB, UK.

ISBN 978-1-84969-522-0

www.packtpub.com

Cover Image by Suresh Mogre (suresh.mogre.99@gmail.com)

Credits

About the Authors

Abhishek Nalwaya is the author of the book, *Rhomobile Beginner's Guide*. He is a Ruby enthusiast and loves to participate regularly at Ruby and Ruby on Rails meetup groups. He works for Mckinsey and Company IT. He has spoken at many conferences, meetups, and was the speaker at RubyConf India 2012 and RubyMotion Conference 2013.

Akshat Paul is a programmer and is working as a lead developer at Mckinsey and Company IT. He has extensive experience of mobile application development and has delivered many enterprise and consumer applications.

In other avatars, Akshat frequently speaks and evangelizes at conferences and meetup groups on various technologies; this way he plays his part in giving back to the community. He has given talks at RubyConfIndia and #inspect-RubyMotion Conference. He also has a strong belief in Agile methodologies for creating world-class software, and is a Certified Scrum Master (CSM).

Acknowledgement

We would like to thank our families and friends, especially Manu Singhal, who saw us through this book, provided support, talked things over, read, wrote, and offered comments, without which conceiving this book wouldn't have been possible.

Also, we would like to thank Usha, Anugya, the entire team at Packt Publishing, and specially Joel Noronha who allowed us to quote their remarks and assisted in the editing, proofreading, and design of this book. Writing a book is a long and arduous journey, but you all made it so easy for us.

About the Reviewers

Florian Bertholin is a software engineer and lead developer. After having studied Computer Sciences in France and in the USA, he now lives in Geneva, Switzerland.

He has been working with Ruby since 2009, and he loves to design High-Scalable Architectures and High-Performance Web Applications.

You can find him online at http://florianbertholin.com.

Vladimir Pouzanov is a systems engineer and mobile development enthusiast. Vladimir spent countless hours hacking different mobile hardware, porting Linux to Palm® devices, and toying outside the iPhone sandbox. He has been doing professional iOS development and consultancy since the first Apple iPhones were available. Later on, Vladimir switched his professional interest to systems management and engineering, but he keeps a close eye on the mobile and embedded world of iPhones, Android devices, and Arduino-based gadgets.

I would like to acknowledge the team of the Hack&Dev project, which brought me to the world of microcontrollers and specifically, Dmitry Shaposhnik for pushing me towards the magic of the Ruby language.

www.PacktPub.com

Support files, eBooks, discount offers and more

You might want to visit www.PacktPub.com for support files and downloads related to your book.

Did you know that Packt offers eBook versions of every book published, with PDF and ePub files available? You can upgrade to the eBook version at www.PacktPub.com and as a print book customer, you are entitled to a discount on the eBook copy. Get in touch with us at service@packtpub.com for more details.

At www.PacktPub.com, you can also read a collection of free technical articles, sign up for a range of free newsletters and receive exclusive discounts and offers on Packt books and eBooks.

http://PacktLib.PacktPub.com

Do you need instant solutions to your IT questions? PacktLib is Packt's online digital book library. Here, you can access, read and search across Packt's entire library of books.

Why Subscribe?
- Fully searchable across every book published by Packt
- Copy and paste, print and bookmark content
- On demand and accessible via web browser

Free Access for Packt account holders

If you have an account with Packt at www.PacktPub.com, you can use this to access PacktLib today and view nine entirely free books. Simply use your login credentials for immediate access.

Table of Contents

Preface

With the arrival of the iOS family of devices, the direction of software development has radically changed. Today people are spending considerable amounts of time on smart devices instead of PCs, which is generating an unprecedented amount of revenue that no industry has ever seen. Despite this, it still fits in your pocket.

So far the application development scene for the iOS ecosystem has been dominated by Objective-C. However, with the introduction of the revolutionary RubyMotion tool chain, Ruby developers are no longer outcasts for creating pure native iOS applications. They can make use of every bit of the all-powerful iOS SDK; and the best part is this can be done without using Xcode.

Both Ruby and RubyMotion are the brainchild of folks who wanted to simplify things in a complex world. *Yukihiro Matsumoto* (also known as *Matz*) is credited for creating the Ruby programming language, which is often regarded as a developer's best friend. And *Laurent Sansonetti* is credited for creating the ground-breaking tool chain, RubyMotion.

RubyMotion iOS Development Essentials will appeal to a developer's mind, especially to the technocrats looking for a reliable tool chain for iOS development. This book] is a step-by-step guide to build an iOS application from scratch to deployment.

What this book covers

Chapter 1, Getting Ready for RubyMotion, gets you acquainted with RubyMotion. Here, we will start with an introduction to RubyMotion, followed by detailed installation steps.

Chapter 2, Instant Gratification – Your First Application, explains how to create a simple Hello World application and also the structure of RubyMotion applications in general.

Chapter 3, *Evolution – From Objective-C to RubyMotion*, helps you understand the journey from Objective-C to RubyMotion. This chapter is also a quick guide to understanding the RubyMotion syntax corresponding to its Objective-C syntax.

Chapter 4, *Mastering MVC Paradigm*, focuses on writing better code with the Model-View-Controller architecture. We will also learn about connecting the application to an external API.

Chapter 5, *User Interface – Cosmetics for Your App*, describes how the user interface is a key part of an iOS application. Also, this chapter explains how we can use the various user interface elements.

Chapter 6, *Device Capability – Power Unleashed*, teaches you how to use various device capabilities, such as Camera, Location Manager, Gestures, Core Data, and Address Book. We will create sample applications for each one of them to understand them better.

Chapter 7, *Interface Builder and WebView – More Goodies!*, explains how to use the interface builder and `UIWebView` with RubyMotion applications.

Chapter 8, *Testing – Let's Fail Gracefully*, discusses Unit Testing and Functional Testing in a RubyMotion application by following the philosophy of Test-driven Development.

Chapter 9, *Creating a Game Application*, helps you create a popular arcade game, Whack-a-Mole, using Cocoa2D and RubyMotion. This is one of the most exciting and unique features of working with RubyMotion where it's possible to create graphical gaming applications.

Chapter 10, *Getting Ready for the App Store*, explains the process of submitting a RubyMotion application to the Apple App Store.

Chapter 11, *Extending RubyMotion*, describes how to augment our RubyMotion applications by making use of the already available open source gems, such as TeaCup, BubbleWrap, and Address Book.

What you need for this book

To program with RubyMotion, firstly you require a Macintosh computer. Since RubyMotion is proprietary software, you are required to buy its license from http://sites.fastspring.com/hipbyte/product/rubymotion.

Who this book is for

This book is for developers who are well versed with the Ruby programming language, and are interested in developing native iOS applications. We do not expect you to have any prior knowledge of RubyMotion. With RubyMotion iOS development essentials, we will discover features of this amazing tool chain from beginner to pro level.

Prior knowledge of Objective-C and the iOS SDK can come in handy at times, but no worries, we have covered every little detail to make you a maven by the end of this book.

Conventions

In this book, you will find a number of styles of text that distinguish between different kinds of information. Here are some examples of these styles, and an explanation of their meaning.

Code words in text, database table names, folder names, filenames, file extensions, pathnames, dummy URLs, user input, and Twitter handles are shown as follows: "Create a `contact_us_controller.rb` file inside the `app` folder."

A block of code is set as follows:

```
@submit_button.addTarget(self,
        action:''send_message'', forControlEvents:UIControlEventT
ouchUpInside)
```

When we wish to draw your attention to a particular part of a code block, the relevant lines or items are set in bold:

```
def setupNavigationBar
  back= UIBarButtonItem.alloc.initWithTitle(''Back'', style:UIBarButto
nItemStylePlain,target:nil ,action:nil)
  self.navigationItem.backBarButtonItem = back;
  contact_us_button = UIBarButtonItem.alloc.initWithTitle(""Contact
Us"", style:UIBarButtonItemStylePlain ,target:self, action:""contact_
us"")
  self.navigationItem.rightBarButtonItem = contact_us_button
end
def contact_us
  contact_us_controller = ContactUsController.alloc.initWithNibName(""
ViewController"", bundle:nil)
  presentModalViewController(contact_us_controller, animated:true)
end
```

Any command-line input or output is written as follows:

```
$rake
```

New terms and **important words** are shown in bold. Words that you see on the screen, in menus or dialog boxes, for example, appear in the text like this: "Open Xcode and click on **Create a new Xcode Project**."

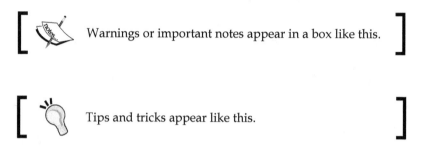

> Warnings or important notes appear in a box like this.

> Tips and tricks appear like this.

Reader feedback

Feedback from our readers is always welcome. Let us know what you think about this book—what you liked or may have disliked. Reader feedback is important for us to develop titles that you really get the most out of.

To send us general feedback, simply send an e-mail to feedback@packtpub.com, and mention the book title via the subject of your message.

If there is a topic that you have expertise in and you are interested in either writing or contributing to a book, see our author guide on www.packtpub.com/authors.

Customer support

Now that you are the proud owner of a Packt book, we have a number of things to help you to get the most from your purchase.

Downloading the example code

You can download the example code files for all Packt books you have purchased from your account at http://www.packtpub.com. If you purchased this book elsewhere, you can visit http://www.packtpub.com/support and register to have the files e-mailed directly to you.

Errata

Although we have taken every care to ensure the accuracy of our content, mistakes do happen. If you find a mistake in one of our books—maybe a mistake in the text or the code—we would be grateful if you would report this to us. By doing so, you can save other readers from frustration and help us improve subsequent versions of this book. If you find any errata, please report them by visiting http://www.packtpub. com/submit-errata, selecting your book, clicking on the **errata submission form** link, and entering the details of your errata. Once your errata are verified, your submission will be accepted and the errata will be uploaded on our website, or added to any list of existing errata, under the Errata section of that title. Any existing errata can be viewed by selecting your title from http://www.packtpub.com/support.

Piracy

Piracy of copyright material on the Internet is an ongoing problem across all media. At Packt, we take the protection of our copyright and licenses very seriously. If you come across any illegal copies of our works, in any form, on the Internet, please provide us with the location address or website name immediately so that we can pursue a remedy.

Please contact us at copyright@packtpub.com with a link to the suspected pirated material.

We appreciate your help in protecting our authors, and our ability to bring you valuable content.

Questions

You can contact us at questions@packtpub.com if you are having a problem with any aspect of the book, and we will do our best to address it.

1

Getting Ready for RubyMotion

"You will never win if you never begin."

–Helen Rowland

Welcome to **RubyMotion iOS** development essentials. The goal of this book is to quickly acquaint you with RubyMotion and start building applications for your favorite iOS device. Ever since the introduction of the first iPhone, followed by the iPad, iOS devices have become very popular because of the way they have revolutionized how people work, and thereby have begun an era of increased productivity. The success behind the phenomenal growth of these devices lies in the applications bundled with them, which increases their functionality exponentially.

We will learn how to develop iOS applications with RubyMotion by building sample applications from scratch. We will try to have something tangible with a running code by the end of every chapter so that you can see a clear progression from chapter to chapter. Though RubyMotion and iOS Cocoa APIs are vast, and part of a fast-moving framework, we'll focus on the smaller, more stable set of core RubyMotion techniques that have crystallized after its release. This means that the knowledge you gain here will not become obsolete quickly. This book is written keeping the Zero-to-Deployment approach in mind.

In this chapter we will learn:

- Various ways to create iOS applications
- How RubyMotion is different from other frameworks
- RubyMotion installation

How can I develop an iOS application?

To develop iOS applications, there are various third-party frameworks available, apart from Apple libraries. If we broadly categorize the ways in which we can create iOS applications, we can divide them into three ways.

Native apps using Objective-C

This is the most standard way to build your application, by interacting with Apple APIs and writing apps in **Objective-C**. Applications made using native Apple APIs can use all possible device capabilities, and are relatively more reliable and high performing (however, the topic of performance is debatable based on the quality of the developer's code).

Mobile web applications

Mobile web applications are simple web applications extended for mobile web browsers, which can be created using standard web technologies such as HTML5. For example, if we browse through `http://www.twitter.com` in a mobile browser, it will be redirected to `http://mobile.twitter.com`, which renders its corresponding views for mobile devices. These applications are easy to create but the downside is that they have limited access to user data (for example, phonebook) and hardware (for example, camera).

Hybrid applications

These applications are somewhere in between mobile web apps and native applications. They are created using common web technologies such as HTML5 and JavaScript and have the ability to use device capabilities via their homegrown APIs. Some of the popular hybrid frameworks include Rhomobile and Phonegap.

If we compare the speed of development and user experience, it can be summed up with the following diagrams:

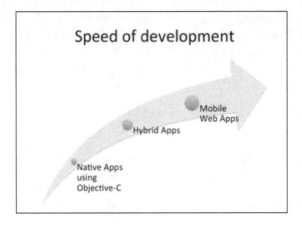

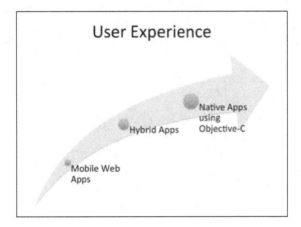

From the preceding diagrams we see that mobile web apps can be created very quickly but we have to compromise on user experience. While native apps using Objective-C have good user experience, they have a very steep initial learning curve for web developers.

RubyMotion is good news for both users and developers. Users get an amazing experience of a native application and developers are able to develop applications rapidly in comparison to applications developed using Objective-C. Let's now learn about RubyMotion.

What is RubyMotion?

RubyMotion is a toolchain that allows developers to develop native iOS applications using the Ruby programming language. RubyMotion acts as a compiler that interacts with the iOS **SDK (Software Development Kit)**. This gives us enormous power to make use of Apple libraries; therefore, once the application has compiled and loaded, the device has no idea whether it's an application made using Objective-C or RubyMotion.

RubyMotion is a product of HipByte, founded by Laurent Sansonetti.

Laurent Sansonetti is a former Apple employee and the brain behind MacRuby. MacRuby is the implementation of Ruby on top of Mac OS X core technologies, which was maintained by Apple for over 4 years. And the best part is that RubyMotion is based on MacRuby.

While developing applications with RubyMotion using Ruby, you always have access to the iOS SDK classes. This gives you the benefit of even mixing Objective-C and Ruby code, as RubyMotion implements Ruby on top of the Objective-C runtime and iOS Foundation classes.

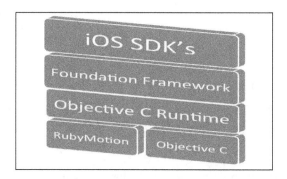

This is how a typical RubyMotion application works. The code written in RubyMotion is fully compiled into machine code, so the application created by RubyMotion is as fast as the one created using Objective-C.

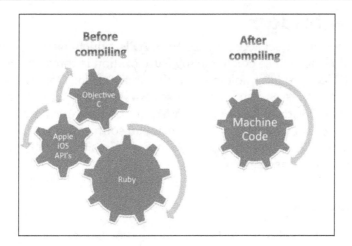

Why RubyMotion?

So far we have learned what RubyMotion is, but the question that comes to mind is, why should we use RubyMotion? There are many reasons why RubyMotion is a good choice for building robust iOS apps. The following sections detail a few that we think matter the most.

If you are not an Objective-C fan

For a newbie developer, Objective-C is an arduous affair. It's complicated to code; even for doing a simple thing, we have to write many lines of code. Though it is a powerful language and one of the best object-oriented ones available, it is time consuming and the learning curve is very steep. On the other hand, Ruby is more expressive, simple, and productive in comparison to Objective-C. Because of its simplicity, developers can shift their focus onto problem solving rather than spending time on trivial stuff, which is taken care by Ruby itself. In short, we can say RubyMotion allows us to use the power of Objective-C with the simplicity of Ruby.

Ruby classes used in RubyMotion are inherited from Objective-C classes. If you are familiar with the concept of object-oriented programming, you can understand its power. This means we can directly use Apple iOS SDK classes from your RubyMotion code. We will be discussing more on this in the next chapter.

 Ruby classes in RubyMotion have the same ancestor as Objective-C.

It is not a bridge

RubyMotion apps get direct access to iOS SDK APIs, which means the size of application and performance created using RubyMotion is comparable to the one created using Objective-C. It implements Ruby on top of the Objective-C runtime and iOS Foundation classes. RubyMotion uses a state-of-the-art static compiler based on **Low Level Virtual Machine (LLVM)**, which converts the Ruby source code into a blazing fast machine code. The original source code is never present in the application bundle. A typical application weighs less than 1 MB, but the size can increase depending on the use case.

Managed memory

One of the key features of RubyMotion is that it takes care of memory management. Just like **ARC (Automatic Reference Counting)** with Xcode 4.4 and above, we don't have to take the pain of releasing the memory once an object is no longer used. RubyMotion does the magic and we don't need to think about it. It handles it on its own.

Terminal-based workflow

RubyMotion has a terminal-based workflow; from creation of the application to deployment, everything can be done through terminals. If you are used to working on terminals, you know it adds to speedier development.

Easy debugging with REPL

The terminal window where you run Rake also gives you the option to debug with **REPL (Read Evaluate Print Loop)**, which lets you use Ruby expressions that are evaluated on the spot, and the results are reflected on the simulator while the application is still running. The ability to make live changes to the user interface and internal application data structures at runtime is extremely useful for testing and troubleshooting issues with the application, as this saves a lot of time and is much faster than a traditional **edit-compile-run** loop. If this confuses you right now, don't worry, as we will discuss more on this powerful feature in later chapters.

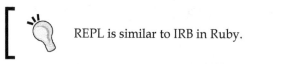

REPL is similar to IRB in Ruby.

It is extendable

We can use RubyMotion salted gems easily by just adding them in the `Rakefile`. What are RubyMotion salted gems? We can't use all the gems that are available for Ruby right now, but there are a lot of gems specifically developed for RubyMotion. As the RubyMotion developer community expands, so will its gem bouquet, and this will make our application development rapid.

Third-party Objective-C libraries can be easily used in a RubyMotion project. It supports CocoaPods, which is a dependency manager for Objective-C libraries, making this process a bit easier.

Debugging and testing

RubyMotion has a console-based inbuilt interactive debugger for troubleshooting the issues both on a simulator and on a device using **GDB (GNU Debugger)**. GDB is extremely powerful on its own, and RubyMotion uses it for debugging the compiled Ruby code. Also, RubyMotion projects are fit for Test Driven Development (TDD). We can write a unit test for our code from the beginning. We can use Behavior Driven Development (BDD) with RubyMotion, which is integrated into every project. We will discuss more about testing in later chapters.

 RubyMine editor also supports RubyMotion and it has a very powerful debugging mechanism through breakpoints.

Pop quiz

Q.1. How can we distinguish between the iOS application created by RubyMotion and the iOS application created by Objective-C?

1. You can distinguish based on the user experience of the application.
2. You can distinguish based on the performance of the application.
3. You can't distinguish based on the user experience and performance of the application.

    Solution: If your answer was option 3, you were right. We can't distinguish between applications created by RubyMotion or Objective-C as the user experience and performance are similar.

Q.2. How can we extend RubyMotion?

1. We can use Objective-C libraries.
2. We can use all Ruby gems.
3. We can use RubyMotion-flavored gems.
4. We can't use any other libraries.

Solution: If your answer was option 1 and 3, you were right. Yes, we can use Objective-C libraries and also RubyMotion-flavored gems.

RubyMotion installation – furnish your environment

Now that we have got a good introduction to RubyMotion, let's set up our development environment; but before that let's run through some of the prerequisites.

Prerequisites for RubyMotion

- You need a Mac OS: we can't develop iOS applications with RubyMotion on any other operating system; so we definitely need a Mac OS.

- OSX 10.6 or higher: RubyMotion requires a Mac running OSX 10.6 or higher. OSX 10.7 Lion is highly recommended.

- Ruby: the Ruby framework comes preinstalled with Mac OS X. If you have multiple versions of Ruby, we recommend that you use **Ruby Version Manager (RVM)**. For more details, visit https://rvm.io/.

- Xcode: next we need to install Xcode, which includes the iOS SDK, developed by Apple and essential for developing iOS applications. It can be downloaded from the App Store for free. It also includes the iPhone/iPad simulator, which will be used for testing our application.

- **Command Line Tools**: after installing the Xcode toolchain, we need to install the command-line tools package, which is necessary for RubyMotion. To confirm that command-line tools is installed with your Xcode, open Xcode in your Applications folder, go to the **Preferences** window, and click on the **Downloads** tab. You should see the **Command Line Tools** package in this list. If it is not yet installed, make sure to click on the **Install** button.

> If you have an old version of Xcode, run the following command on the terminal:
>
> ```
> sudo xcode-select -switch /Applications/Xcode.app/
> Contents/Developer
> ```
>
> This command will set up the default Xcode path.

Installing RubyMotion

RubyMotion installation is really simple and takes no time at all. RubyMotion is a commercial product that you need to purchase from www.rubymotion.com. Once purchased, you will receive your unique license key and installer.

RubyMotion installation is a five-step procedure and is given here:

1. Once you have received the package, run the RubyMotion installer as follows:

2. Read and accept the **EULA (End User License Agreement)**.

3. Enter the license number you have received as shown in the following screenshot:

4. Time for a short break—it will take a few minutes for RubyMotion to get downloaded and installed on your system. You can relax for some time.

5. Yippee!! There is no step 5. And that's how quick it is to start working with RubyMotion.

Update RubyMotion

RubyMotion is a fast-moving framework and we need to upgrade it once there is a new release available. Upgrading RubyMotion is again really simple—with one command, you can easily upgrade it to the latest version.

```
sudo motion update
```

You need to be connected to the Internet for an upgrade to happen.

> If you want to work on an old version, you can downgrade using the following command:
>
> ```
> sudo motion update -force-version=1.2
> ```
>
> But we recommend using the latest version.

How do we check we've done everything correctly?

Now that we have installed our RubyMotion copy, it's good practice to confirm which version we have installed; to do this, go to the terminal and run the following:

```
motion -v
```

This command outputs the RubyMotion version installed on your machine. If you get an error, you need to reinstall.

Pick your own editor – you are not forced to use Xcode

With RubyMotion, you are not forced to use Xcode. As every developer is more comfortable with a specific editor, you are open to choose what you like. However, we recommend the following editors for Ruby development:

- RubyMine
- Vim
- TextMate
- Sublime
- Emacs

> RubyMine now provides full support to a RubyMotion project.

How to get help

If you are facing some issues, the preferred way to get a solution is to discuss it at the RubyMotion Google group, (`https://groups.google.com/forum/?fromgroups#!forum/rubymotion`), where you can interact with fellow developers from the community and get a speedy resolution.

Sometimes you might not get a precise response from the RubyMotion group. Not to worry, RubyMotion support is there to rescue you. If you have a feature request, an issue, or simply want to ask a question, you can log a support ticket—that too from the command line using the following command:

```
$ motion support
```

This will open up a new window in your browser. You can fill and submit the form with your query. Your RubyMotion license key, email address, and environment details will be added automatically.

The RubyMotion community is growing at a very fast pace. In a short span of time, a lot of popular RubyMotion gems have been created by developers.

FAQs

We believe no question is silly. By now you will have many questions in your mind regarding RubyMotion. We have tried to answer a few of the most frequently asked questions (FAQs) related to topics covered so far in this section. Here are a few of them:

Q1. Are the applications created by RubyMotion in keeping with Apple guidelines?

Answer. Yes, RubyMotion strongly follows the review guidelines provided by Apple. Many applications created using RubyMotion are already available at the App Store.

Q2. Will my RubyMotion application work on a Blackberry, Android, or Windows phone?

Answer. No, applications created using RubyMotion are only for iOS devices; it is an alternative to programming in Objective-C. For a single-source multi-device application, we would recommend hybrid frameworks such as Rhomobile, Phonegap, and Titanium. For android development using Ruby, you can try Rubuto.

Q3. Can I share an application with someone?

Answer. Yes and no. With the Apple Developer Program membership, you can share your application only for testing purposes with a maximum of 100 devices, where each device has to be registered individually with Apple. Also, you cannot distribute your application on the App Store for testing. Once you have finished developing your application and are ready to ship, you can submit it to Apple for an App Store review.

Q4. Can I use Ruby gems?

Answer. Yes and no. No because we can't use normal Ruby gems, which you generally use in your Ruby on Rails projects; and yes because you can use gems that are specifically developed for RubyMotion, and there are already many such gems.

Q5. Will my application work on iPad and iPod Touch?

Answer. Absolutely, your application will work on any iOS devices, namely iPhone, iPad, and iPod Touch.

Q6 Is Ruby allowed on the App Store?

Answer. The App Store can't distinguish between applications made using Objective-C and those made using RubyMotion. So, no worries, our RubyMotion applications are fit for the App Store.

Q7. Can I use third-party Objective-C libraries?

Answer. Certainly. Third-party Objective-C libraries can be used in your project. RubyMotion provides integration with the CocoaPods dependency manager, which helps in reducing the hassle. You also can use C/C++ code provided that you wrap it into the Objective-C classes and methods.

Q8. Is RubyMotion open source?

Answer. RubyMotion as a toolchain is open source (available at GitHub). The closed source part is the Ruby runtime, which is, however, very similar to MacRuby runtime (which is open source).

Summary

Before we move to the next chapter, let's review all that we have learned so far. We first discussed the different ways to create iOS applications. Then we started with RubyMotion and discussed why to use it. And in the last section, we learned how to get started with RubyMotion and which editor fits with it.

Now that we have our RubyMotion framework up and running, the next obvious task is to create our very first application, the most rudimentary `Hello World` application. In the next chapter, we will also learn the structure of the RubyMotion application in general.

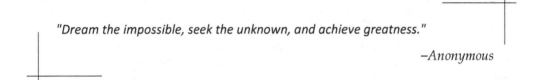

Instant Gratification – Your First Application

"Dream the impossible, seek the unknown, and achieve greatness."

–Anonymous

Now that we are all charged up about RubyMotion and have our system set up, let's create a simple RubyMotion application. We will try and keep it simple, but sometimes you may feel disconnected by monotonously typing the code. Although, going along is enough for now. Remember that mimicry is a powerful form of learning; that's how we have learned most of our skills, such as talking, reading, writing, and that is how you will learn to program with RubyMotion. We promise you that by the end of this book, you will have sufficient knowledge of RubyMotion to create an iOS application and make it live on the App Store. In this chapter we will cover the following topics:

- Creating your first RubyMotion application
- Understanding the folder structure
- Exploring the command line
- Configuring your application
- REPL – the interactive console
- The debugger

Your first application

Let's start with the classic `HelloWorld` application. As we have discussed in the last chapter, RubyMotion has a terminal-based flow, so let's fire up our terminal and create our very first RubyMotion application.

```
$motion create HelloWorld
Create HelloWorld
    Create HelloWorld/.gitignore
    Create HelloWorld/Rakefile
    Create HelloWorld/app
    Create HelloWorld/app/app_delegate.rb
    Create HelloWorld/resources
    Create HelloWorld/spec
    Create HelloWorld/spec/main_spec.rb
```

If you observe closely the output on the terminal screen, you will see that a lot of files and directories have been generated by a single `motion` command, which automatically creates standard directories, and you will also see the file structure that will quickly bring us onboard with app development, which we can work on later and enhance to make a fully functional application. Moreover, since the structure is common to all the RubyMotion apps, it's easy to understand.

 Just like the `motion` command, popular frameworks such as Ruby on Rails also have commands such as `rails` to create a predefined layout of the application.

The following steps automatically compile the code and start the application on a simulator:

1. Start the application, traverse to the application directory, and type the following command:

```
$ cd HelloWorld
$rake
Build ./build/iPhoneSimulator-6.0-Development
Compile ./app/app_delegate.rb
Create ./build/iPhoneSimulator-6.0-Development/HelloWorld.app
Link ./build/iPhoneSimulator-6.0-Development/HelloWorld.app/
HelloWorld
Create ./build/iPhoneSimulator-6.0-Development/HelloWorld.app/
Info.plist
Create ./build/iPhoneSimulator-6.0-Development/HelloWorld.app/
PkgInfo
```

```
Create ./build/iPhoneSimulator-6.0-Development/HelloWorld.dSYM
warning: no debug symbols in executable (-arch i386)
Simulate ./build/iPhoneSimulator-6.0-Development/HelloWorld.app
```

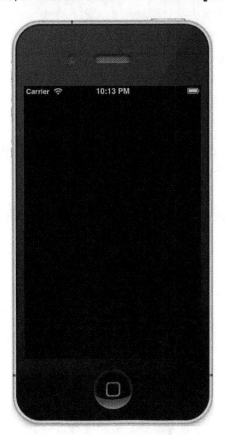

Wow! The `rake` command automatically compiles the code and starts the application on a simulator. So far, we have not created any views for our application; that's why we can see a blank screen. It looks boring, but remember that we have not written a single line of code. So let's write some code, create some views, and build our application again.

 You can open the RubyMotion project in your favorite editor. If you don't have an editor yet, you can use either TextEdit or VIM.

2. Open the file `app_delegate.rb` in the app folder and add the following code in it:

```
class AppDelegate
  def application(application, didFinishLaunchingWithOptions:launc
hOptions)
    alert = UIAlertView.new
    alert.message = "Hello World!"
    alert.show
    true
  end
end
```

3. Let's re-run our application by traversing to the application directory and typing the execute command (`rake`):

$rake

The `rake` command will compile our code and fire up the iPhone simulator. We can see a blue pop-up saying **Hello World!** in the following screenshot:

Let's understand the code that we have written in AppDelegate. Here the application method (didFinishLaunchingWithOptions:launchOptions) is called first when our application starts. This will be the starting point of our application and the right place to define our window.

RubyMotion functions are a combination of the usual Ruby name method (didFinishLaunchingWithOptions) with their named parameters; a variable directly follows the function, which it refers to, and therefore, we don't need to know the implementation of the function.

> Named parameters were added to RubyMotion to preserve the existing Objective-C APIs, and the extra symbols are required parts of the method name, for example, didFinishLaunchingWithOptions:launchOptions.

As discussed, the code written in AppDelegate will be called automatically as the application is initialized.

In the following code snippet, we created an object alert of the UIAlertView class and then we assigned a Hello World! string to the message attribute of the object. Now we have our alert object ready. To display this alert on the device screen, we call the show method on the alert object as follows:

```
alert = UIAlertView.new
alert.message = "Hello World!"
alert.show
```

UIAlertView is a class that is bundled in the UIKit framework of the iOS. We can use this class to display an alert message on the screen. This class is inherited from UIView that is inherited from UIResponder that, in turn, is inherited from NSObject.

Why do we see the NS prefix?

Objective-C is a superset of C and thus doesn't have namespaces like in C++; therefore, the symbols must be prefixed with a unique prefix so that they don't collide. This is particularly important for symbols defined in a framework. The original code for the Cocoa frameworks came from the NextStep libraries, and so the NextStep engineers chose to prefix their symbols with NS.

4. To exit the application, close the simulator by selecting the **exit** option or press *Command + Q*.

The iOS simulator is a great tool for testing your applications quickly. It comes bundled with Xcode. But you can't test everything on the simulator. To test the shaking of a device, camera, GPS, Accelerometer, Gyroscope, and other device capabilities, you may require additional products to pass device data to the app in the simulator.

Folder structure

In this section, we will understand the folder structure of our application as we know from the previous section that `motion create <project name>` sets up the directory structure with all the essential files to run a simple RubyMotion application. Let's walk through each one of them to have a precise understanding of their function:

- The `app` folder: This is the core of your application code; you will write most of your code in this folder. RubyMotion iterates in this folder and loads any `.rb` file that it catches.

If you want to keep your code somewhere else other than the `app` directory, add the folder path to the `Rakefile`.

- The `app_delegate.rb` file in the `app` folder: This file is at the heart of the RubyMotion application. If you are a little familiar with iOS development, this is the delegate file. A delegate is an object that usually reacts to some event in another object and/or can affect how another object behaves. There are various methods that can be implemented in `UIApplicationDelegate`. These methods are called during the different phases of an application, such as during the finish of its launch, during termination, when the application is low on memory, and during the occurrence of important changes. While the application is running, tracking its state transitions is one of the main jobs of the application delegate.

  App delegates use the method `application:didFinishLaunchingWithOpt ions` as the first entry point. This method is called after your application has been launched. When this method is called, your application is in the inactive state. A few other methods available are:

  - ° `applicationWillEnterForeground`
  - ° `applicationWillTerminate`
  - ° `application:shouldSaveApplicationState`
  - ° `application:shouldRestoreApplicationState`

A full list of available methods can be obtained from the iOS developer library (http://developer.apple.com/library/ios). The good part here is that most of the methods are self-explanatory by their name. For example, applicationWillEnterForeground will be called when your application is relaunched.

> We see that in some iOS 6 applications, the app is restored to the previous state; we can handle this in an application delegate.

- The resources folder: As the name suggests, the resources folder contains static content, such as images, sounds, UI layouts, and icons that we use in our applications.

- The Spec folder: This folder contains automated test cases. RubyMotion supports a Ruby testing framework, Bacon; it is a small RSpec clone that is used for writing unit, functional, and UI tests. By default, it creates main_spec.rb as an example.

- Rakefile: With Rakefile we can configure our application name, resources, gems to be included, and the code location. We will discuss more about Rakefile later in this chapter.

Some more goodies

We know that it's not so much fun to have only a simple HelloWorld pop-up as our very first application, so let's jazz up our code by adding some more goodies to our alert box; and this time, let's do things in a much better way.

Earlier we had added an alert box in the delegate itself. Actually it is not a good idea to write code in the application delegate. It is better to write code in a Model-View-Controller (MVC) way. Right now we won't cover all three parts of the MVC architecture for now let's begin with the controller for our application and add three buttons in this alert box, add a title, and add a message for the title box.

The class UIAlertView that we've used in the last section has numerous properties, such as title, message, delegate, cancelButtonTitle, otherButtonTitles, and many more. Let's use a few of them in our application as follows:

1. Create a file root_controller.rb in the app folder and add the following code:

```
class RootController < UIViewController
    def viewDidLoad
    alert = UIAlertView.alloc.initWithTitle "This is foo title",
```

```
        message:"Do you like this example?",
          delegate: nil,
          cancelButtonTitle: "cancel"
          otherButtonTitles: "Yes","No",nil
      alert.show
      end
  end
```

2. To call this controller, we need to update our `AppDelegate` class. Replace the following code in your `app_delegate.rb` file:

```
class AppDelegate
  def application
    (application,didFinishLaunchingWithOptions:
      launchOptions)
    @window = UIWindow.alloc.initWithFrame
      (UIScreen.mainScreen.bounds)
    @window.rootViewController = RootController.alloc.init
    @window.rootViewController.wantsFullScreenLayout = true
    @window.makeKeyAndVisible
    true
  end
end
```

3. Start the simulator by running the `rake` command from the console inside your application directory as follows:

That's cool; our earlier `HelloWorld` pop-up has now been replaced with an alert box that has a title, a cancel button, and two other buttons.

 The iOS SDK has been built around the MVC pattern that separates responsibilities and ends up with an application that is easy to design and maintain.

Let's understand the code

When an iPhone application starts, it puts a window on the screen, which we have created using the `UIWindow` class. You can think of a window as a drawing board where you can put anything, such as a button, textbox or label. The instance of the `UIWindow` class manages and coordinates the views of an application, which are displayed on a device screen.

A `UIScreen` object contains the bounding rectangle of the device's entire screen. So, `UIScreen.mainScreen.bounds` returns the rectangle size according to the screen size and orientation of the device.

 Every iOS application needs at least one window, which is an instance of the `UIWindow` class.

You might be wondering, should I remember all the properties and methods of the Apple iOS SDK, such as `UIAlertView`? It is not necessary to memorize them as one can always refer to the properties and methods from the iOS development library. Nevertheless, having a basic idea about the usage of a class can come in handy at times. The popular IDE, RubyMine, supports RubyMotion. It also has a useful autocompletion feature.

 The more you understand, the less you have to memorize.

Exploring the command line

RubyMotion is based on an underlying principle, "to use the tools which developers love". Therefore, to create an application using RubyMotion, we require only two tools; the first is your favorite editor and the second is the terminal. While developing a RubyMotion application, you will be required to familiarize yourself with the command line. Familiarity with the terminal always helps in faster and comfortable development.

Now that we have created our `HelloWorld` application, let us explore a few commands that we have already used, and remember that RubyMotion uses them considerably. These commands are responsible for inaugurating our RubyMotion projects, `motion` and `rake`.

Motion command – one-stopshop

As used previously, the `motion` command creates our RubyMotion project and also supports various other options. The `motion` command is similar to the popular framework Ruby on Rails' `rails` command. Before we go any further, let's fire up our terminal and see what can be done using the `motion` command.

```
$ motion
Usage:
  motion [-h, --help]
  motion [-v, --version]
  motion <command> [<args...>]
Commands:
  account      Access the software license account
  activate     Activate the software license
  create       Create a new project
  ri           Display API reference
  update       Update the software
  support      Create a support ticket
```

- `motion account`: This displays the account/license information on the browser.

- `motion activate`: If you want to activate your RubyMotion framework with a new license or if you have not yet activated the framework, `motion activate` can be used.

- `motion create <project name>`: This command will generate a RubyMotion project's skeleton that will have all the essential files needed to begin developing an iOS application.

- `motion ri <API-name>`: This command helps us to find the documentation for the API that has been mentioned.

- `motion update`: RubyMotion is a fast-moving framework and often requires updates. `motion update` updates your framework from the command line itself.

- `motion support`: There may be times when you have questions only an expert can answer. `motion support` helps you connect with RubyMotion directly, and you can ask a question by filling up a form. It can also be used for any feature request or for reporting a bug.

Rake tasks – get things done fast

Rake is a simple Ruby build program with capabilities similar to `Make`. RubyMotion's `rake` command has many predefined tasks that help you do several trivial jobs, such as compiling your code to test in a simulator or creating a package to test on a device, with ease. Let's fire up our terminal again and check what tasks can be performed using `rake --tasks`.

```
$ rake --tasks
```

The following table elaborates the different Rake tasks:

Rake task	Description
Rake archive	Create a `.ipa` archive
Rake archive:distribution	Create a `.ipa` archive for distribution
Rake build	Build everything
Rake build:device	Build the device version
Rake build:simulator	Build the simulator version
Rake clean	Clear build objects
Rake config	Show project config
Rake ctags	Generate ctags
Rake default	Build the project, then run the simulator
Rake device	Deploy on the device
Rake simulator	Run the simulator
Rake spec	Same as a `spec:simulator`
Rake spec:device	Run the test/spec suite on the device
Rake spec:simulator	Run the test/spec suite on the simulator
Rake static	Create a static library

So Rake has plenty of tasks to do, but most importantly, out of all these tasks, if we simply run Rake, it will build and run our application on the iOS simulator.

Rake file – configuring your application

RubyMotion applications are highly configurable using different attributes in a `Rakefile`. These attributes, by default, come with a sensible value but can be overridden with custom values. Let's explore each one of them—this section will come in handy, time and again, as we proceed with our application.

To see your current application configuration, run the `rake config` task, and you will be presented with the following list:

```
$ rake config
background_modes        : []
build_dir               : "./build"
codesign_certificate    : "Error"
delegate_class          : "AppDelegate"
deployment_target       : "6.0"
device_family           : :iphone
entitlements            : {}
files                   : ["./app/app_delegate.rb", "./app/twitter.rb",
"./app/twitter_controller.rb"]
fonts                   : []
frameworks              : ["UIKit", "Foundation", "CoreGraphics",
"CoreGraphics"]
icons                   : []
identifier              : "com.yourcompany.MacBaconUI"
interface_orientations  : [:portrait, :landscape_left, :landscape_right]
libs                    : []
motiondir               : "/Library/RubyMotion"
name                    : "MacBacon UI"
prerendered_icon        : false
provisioning_profile    : "Error"
resources_dir           : "./resources"
sdk_version             : "6.0"
seed_id                 : "Error"
short_version           : "1"
specs_dir               : "./spec"
status_bar_style        : :default
version                 : "1.0"
weak_frameworks         : []
xcode_dir               : "/Applications/Xcode.app/Contents/Developer"
```

You can see the entire configuration settings for your application. These settings can be modified in a `Rakefile`. You may find it easy to understand what these properties do by their names, but let us explain a few of them:

- `name`: This is where you can specify the name of your project as a string. By default, the name of your application will be the attribute that you passed during `motion create`.

- `version`: This variable saves the current application version as a string; it is 1.0 by default.

- `identifier`: The project identifier is a string that is in reverse DNS — a naming convention that is in the reverse order of the domain name notation — such as `com.yourcompany.yourapp`.

- `delegate_class`: This is where you specify your application delegate class as a string that is loaded once the application starts. The default value is `AppDelegate` and the class is defined in the `app/app_delegate.rb` file. However, we can rename the `AppDelegate` class to a custom name of our choice and this then has to be updated in the `Rakefile`.

- `Files`: This shows every `.rb` file in the `app` directory in an array format. The default value is the result of executing the following expression:

  `Dir.glob(./app/*/.rb)`

- `framework`: This shows the names of the iOS frameworks that are used in our application in an array format. Soon you will be using many iOS frameworks, such as CoreFoundation, CoreMotion, and others, with your application. The build system is capable of dealing with dependencies, therefore they should be mentioned here. The default value is either `UIKit`, `Foundation`, or `CoreGraphics`.

- `libs`: This variable shows the library paths that are to be linked to the application in an array format. It contains the path to public system libraries, for example, **/usr/lib/libz.dylib**. The default value is `[]`, an empty array.

- `build_dir`: This variable is used to specify the directory path where you want the application build to be created in a string format. It must be relative to the project directory. The directory initially gets created automatically. In case it is not created, a temporary directory will be used instead. The default value is `build`.

- `resources_dir`: This variable is used to specify the directory for the resource files where all the images and icons go in a string format. It must be relative to the project directory. The default value is `resources`.

- `spec_dir`: This variable is used to specify the directory of `spec` files where all our test cases are present in a String format. The default value is `spec`. It should be relative to the project directory.

- `icons`: This variable lists the icons used for the application present in the `resources` folder in an `array` format, for example, `icon.png` and/or `icon-72.png`. The files should be in tune with Apple's **HIG (Human Interface Guidelines)**. By default, the value is `[]`, an empty array.

- `fonts`: This variable lists the names of the font files present in the `resources` directory in an `array` format. These fonts will be taken into account while either generating the application bundle or testing on a simulator.

- `prerendered_icon`: iOS application icons usually have a reflective shine on them. For that purpose, this property is used. If it is false, we will get the reflective shine on the icon. By default, the value is false.

- `device_family`: With this property, we can specify which family of iOS device our application supports. The values can be `iphone`, `ipad`, or for universal application `[:iphone, :ipad]`. By default it is `:iphone`.

- `interface_orientations`: Apple iOS devices support various orientations for an application. They can be `portrait`, `landscape_left`, `landscape_right`, or `portrait_upside_down`. By default, the value is an array of `:portrait`, `:landscape_left`, or `:landscape_right`.

- `Xcode_dir`: This configuration tells us where the Xcode is installed.

 Giving a new value to the `XCode_dir` property should generally be done first, before changing other `Rakefile` properties.

- `sdk_version`: This configuration lets us decide which SDK version will be used. By default, the value is the most recent version of the supported SDK.

- `deployment_target`: This configuration shows which iOS SDK to target for the RubyMotion project. By default, the value is of the current SDK version that is installed, but this can be changed to any desired version of the iOS SDK, for example, 6.0 that will use iOS SDK Version 6.0.

- `codesign_certificate`: This configuration shows which code-signing certificate is used. By default, the value is the first iPhone developer certificate in the keychain utility; for example, in our case it is **iPhone developer: Paul Akshat (S3KPMT842Z)**.

- `provisioning_profile`: This configuration variable specifies the path of the provisioning profile.

- `seed_id`: The Apple provisioning profile has an identifier. This configuration shows us the same, which is usually the first application identifier picked from the provisioning profile.

REPL – the interactive console

RubyMotion comes with an interactive console that lets us traverse and scan the code that we are using in our application. The good thing is that the console is connected to the application running on the simulator. This means that if we make any changes from the console, it will be reflected on the simulator in real time. Let's try this with our `HelloWorld` application.

Run the application as follows:

$rake

As expected, it will open a simulator and the terminal screen will show:

(main)>

Now hold the *Command* key and hover the mouse over the simulator. You will see a red-bordered box. As we move the mouse pointer over an element, we can see its corresponding class object appearing in the terminal window `(UIView:0xc5710c0)?` as seen in the following screenshot. Now click the mouse to select the object that you want to work on dynamically.

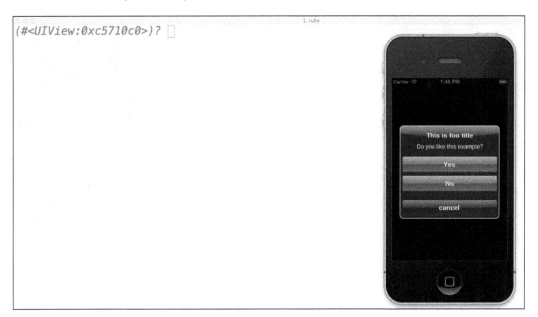

Try the following command on the terminal and observe the changes in the simulator:

`self` returns the current object selected by the mouse.

```
(#<UIView:0x7652680>)> self
=> #<UIView:0x7652680>
```

Create an object `blue` for the `UIColor` class and assign the color blue to the variable as follows:

```
(#<UIView:0x7652680>)> blue = UIColor.blueColor
```

To change the background color of the view, use the `backgroundColor` property of the selected view as follows:

```
=> #<UICachedDeviceRGBColor:0xb05a800>
  (#<UIView:0x7652680>)>  self.backgroundColor = blue
=> #<UICachedDeviceRGBColor:0xb05a800>
```

Make sure that the background color on the simulator has been changed to blue as shown in the following screenshot:

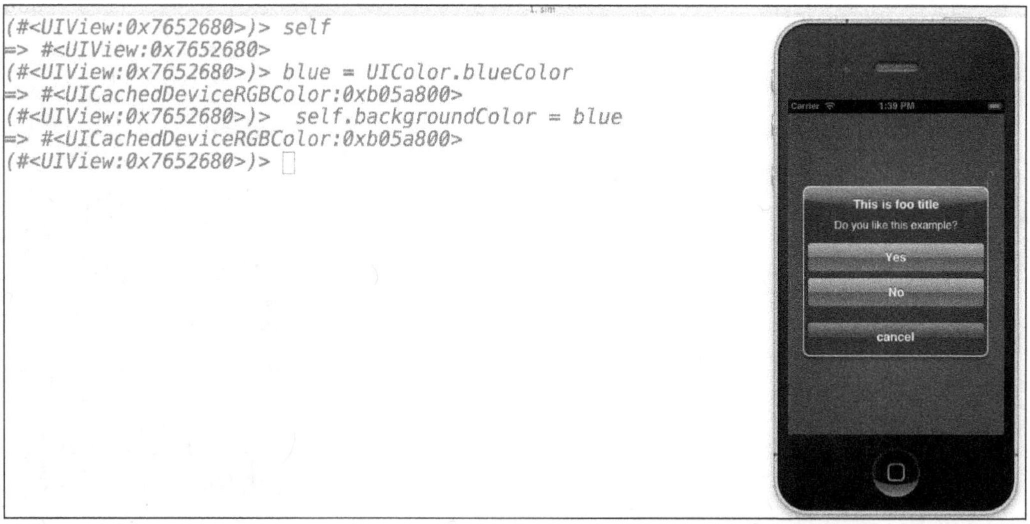

Let's dismiss the alert box by clicking on any button and put a new alert box with the following code:

```
a = UIAlertView.new
a.title = "My Title"
a.message = "Hello World!"
a.show
```

The simulator shows a new alert box on screen without compiling the code as shown in the following screenshot:

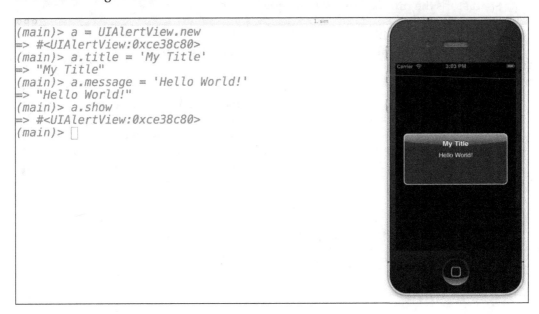

```
(main)> a = UIAlertView.new
=> #<UIAlertView:0xce38c80>
(main)> a.title = 'My Title'
=> "My Title"
(main)> a.message = 'Hello World!'
=> "Hello World!"
(main)> a.show
=> #<UIAlertView:0xce38c80>
(main)> 
```

You can dismiss the alert box as follows:

```
(main) > a.dismiss
```

We can see how REPL is a great tool for developing applications for iOS and how it helps us make changes dynamically. To make these changes permanent we need to add the same code to our source code.

Debugger – catch your mistakes!

A typical debugger provides the ability to halt when specific conditions are encountered. It also offers sophisticated functions, such as running a program step by step, breaking or pausing the program for an examination based on breakpoints, and tracking the values of the variables at that state. RubyMotion Version 1.24 and above support debugging using GDB: the GNU project debugger (http://www.gnu.org/software/gdb/).

The RubyMotion debugger provides the following inbuilt debugging facilities:

- It stops the program at a specific line
- It examines the problem when the program has stopped
- It checks the value for the variables at a specific breakpoint

 The RubyMotion compiler implements the **DWARF** debugging format's metadata for the Ruby language. This allows external programs, such as the debugger in our case, to retrieve source-level information about the RubyMotion application. The metadata is saved under a `.dSYM` bundle file at the same level as the `.app` bundle in the build directory of your project.

How to start debugging

There are three ways in which we can start the debugger.

While testing on a simulator

We can start the debugger with a simulator. The debugger will directly attach itself to the app and replace the interactive shell (REPL).

To start, just type:

```
$rake simulator debug=1
```

While testing on a device

We can start debugging with the device running simultaneously. The build system will start the iOS debugging server on the device and then remotely attach the debugger on your shell right after the application has been deployed on the device.

```
$rake device debug=1
```

In the release mode, local variables might not be accessible in the debugger as they are optimized to fit into CPU registers.

 To test your application on a device, you are required to enroll for the **Apple Developer Program**. We will discuss this in detail in later chapters.

Entering commands before starting

We might need some breakpoint before loading the application; we can do this as follows:

```
$rake debug=1 no_continue=1
```

On execution of this command, the GDB will start and we will be able to set the breakpoints. This is discussed in more detail in the next section.

Breakpoint

We can put breakpoints at a specific location of our application code using the `break` command and then pass the location where the debugger should stop the execution of the code using the `file_name:line_number` notation.

Let's try putting a breakpoint in our current application. To do so, we need to start our `HelloWorld` application in debugging mode as follows:

```
$rake simulator debug=1
/Library/RubyMotion/lib/motion/project/config.rb:89:
    Build ./build/iPhoneSimulator-5.1-Development
  Simulate ./build/iPhoneSimulator-5.1-Development/HelloWorld.app
Attaching to process 86665.
Reading symbols for shared libraries . done
0x8fe6c030 in __dyld__dyld_start ()
Function "rb_exc_raise" not defined.
Breakpoint 1 (rb_exc_raise) pending.
Function "malloc_error_break" not defined.
Breakpoint 2 (malloc_error_break) pending.
Reading symbols for shared libraries ...................................
...........................................................................
. done
Breakpoint 1 at 0x37136
Pending breakpoint 1 - "rb_exc_raise" resolved
Breakpoint 2 at 0x97bdec97
Pending breakpoint 2 - "malloc_error_break" resolved
Reading symbols for shared libraries . done
Reading symbols for shared libraries . done
Reading symbols for shared libraries ... done
(gdb)
```

Now let's set a breakpoint on the eighth line of the file `app_delegate.rb` as follows:

```
(gdb) break app_delegate.rb:8
Breakpoint 3 at 0x80085: file app_delegate.rb, line 8
```

With the preceding command, the execution of your application will halt at line number 8 of the `app_delegate.rb` file.

Listing breakpoints

To list the breakpoints that have been set up in the current debugging environment, we use the `info breakpoint` command as follows:

```
(gdb) info breakpoint
```

Num	Type	Disp	Enb	Address	What
1	breakpoint	keep	y	0x000adff6	<rb_exc_raise+6>
2	breakpoint	keep	y	0x97bdec97	<malloc_error_break+6>
3	breakpoint	keep	y	0x00080085	in rb_scope__application:didFinish

LaunchingWithOptions:__ at app_delegate.rb:8

We can see that the list of breakpoints created in the last section can also be seen in the list.

Moving between the different breakpoints

The `continue` command will continue the execution of the program until it reaches the next breakpoint.

```
(gdb) continue
```

We can also use its alias `c` as follows; it is more handy to use:

```
(gdb) c
Breakpoint 3, rb_scope__application:didFinishLaunchingWithOptions:__
(self=0x9408440, application=0x9401750, launchOptions=0x4) at app_
delegate.rb:8
8       alert.show
```

The `next` command will continue the execution of the program until the next source-level location. This is usually the very next line in the Ruby source code. You should have a look at the terminal for the relevant source code line.

```
(gdb) next
```

Checking the value of a local variable

This is an important feature of debugging, to check the value of a variable at a specific breakpoint.

```
(gdb) pro alert
#<UIAlertView:0x944b9b0>
```

This shows that the alert is an object of the UIAlertView class

Pro (print-ruby-object) accepts two parameters as follows:

- The object on which the variable will be retrieved.
- The variable name that you want to get.

> To check the variables available for us to execute, run the following command:
> ```
> $info locals
> ```

Checking the value of an instance variable

We can also check the value of an instance variable during some breakpoint using **pri (print-ruby-ivar)** as follows:

```
pri self "@tweet"
```

pri accepts two commands as follows:

- The object on which the instance variable will be retrieved.
- The instance variable that you want to get. Make sure to include the @ character in the name.

> You can use pri @tweet instead of pri self @tweet.

Disable breakpoint

To disable a breakpoint, use disable followed by the breakpoint number; it has to be disabled as follows:

```
(gdb) disable 3
```

Exit debugger

Type quit to exit the debugger as follows:

```
(gdb) quit
The program is running.  Quit anyway (and detach it)? (y or n) y
Detaching from process 6792.
```

Downloading the example code

You can download the example code files for all Packt books you have purchased, and the graphics bundle of this book from your account at http://www.packtpub.com.

If you purchased this book elsewhere, you can visit http://www.packtpub.com/support and register to have the files e-mailed directly to you.

Summary

Let's recap what we have done in this chapter:

- Created a simple RubyMotion application
- Discussed the basic RubyMotion application structure
- Explored the commands available with RubyMotion
- Performed different Rake tasks with RubyMotion
- Learned how to configure your RubyMotion application
- Worked with the interactive console—REPL
- Debugged your application using the RubyMotion debugger

In the next chapter, we turn our attention to RubyMotion data type objects—such as strings and arrays. We will also learn how to interface with C and we will focus on memory management in RubyMotion.

3
Evolution – From Objective-C to RubyMotion

"Actually, I'm trying to make Ruby natural, not simple."

— Matz

In this chapter, we will have a detailed discussion on how Ruby is implemented in RubyMotion. We will also understand how we can use the various Objective-C objects in our Ruby code. As we know, the iOS SDK is written in Objective-C, which is a simple extension of the C language. Since this is a book on learning RubyMotion, we will not focus too much on this. However, we will make sure you have enough knowledge on Objective-C to program in RubyMotion. In this chapter, we will cover the following topics:

- How Ruby and Objective-C work together in RubyMotion
- In what ways are RubyMotion objects inherited from Objective-C
- Interfacing with C and Objective-C – learning about data types
- Memory management with RubyMotion

Ruby and Objective-C – a partnership

You must be wondering how Objective-C and Ruby can work together, as Objective-C is a compiled language and Ruby is an interpreted language. Then how come they work together in RubyMotion?

In reality, Objective-C in the iOS SDK not only has a compiler, but also has a runtime system to execute the compiled code. This runtime system acts as an interface for the Objective-C language; this is what makes the language work. RubyMotion takes advantage of the Objective-C runtime and our Ruby code interacts through this runtime system in just the same way as an Objective-C code does. That means Ruby and Objective-C are effectively working on top of the Objective-C runtime.

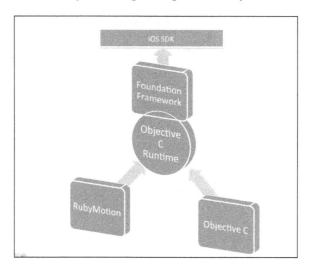

The preceding diagram represents the way RubyMotion and Objective-C work together in an iOS SDK ecosystem. In simple terms, this means we can access all iOS SDK classes with RubyMotion through the Objective-C runtime. The **Foundation Framework** is an Objective-C framework, but the great news is that RubyMotion is, in fact, based on Objective-C runtime; therefore, the classes that are defined can naturally be re-used in RubyMotion.

 The runtime library is written mainly in the C language and is open source. This is available at `http://opensource.apple.com`.

Ruby and Objective-C share the same ancestor

Some of the built-in classes of RubyMotion are based on the Foundation Framework. To better understand this, let's fire up REPL in our console for our existing RubyMotion application from the previous chapter. As you may remember, in that chapter we had learned how to use REPL. Run the `rake` command to start REPL and then run the following commands in REPL:

```
(main) > a = 5
=> 5
(main) > a.class
=> Fixnum
(main) > a.superclass
=> NSNumber
(main) > name = ""Abhishek""
=> ""Abhishek""
(main) > name.class
=> String
(main) > name.superclass
=> NSMutableString
(main) > a.superclass.superclass
=> NSString
(main) > a.superclass.superclass.superclass
=> NSObject
```

In the preceding example, we have found the root for the Ruby `integer` and `string` classes. Firstly, we declared a variable and assigned an integer value to it. When we trace its class, we see a familiar name, `Fixnum`, which is a Ruby data type. But when we trace back to the super class for `Fixnum`, we see that it's an Objective-C Integer type. This shows that the RubyMotion `Fixnum` data type is inherited from `NSNumber`.

Similarly, when we declare a string variable name and then trace its class, we see a recognizable Ruby class, `String`. Moreover, this string class is inherited from `NSMutableString`. This means the `String` Ruby class is a subclass of the Objective-C `String` class in RubyMotion.

A direct consequence of hosting the Ruby built-in classes over Foundation is that their instances respond to more messages. For example, the `NSString` class defines the uppercase `String` method. Since the `String` class is a subclass of `NSString`, strings created in Ruby also respond to that method, as shown here:

```
''hello''.uppercaseString # => ''HELLO''
```

This gives us immense flexibility to not only use Ruby methods, but also access thousands of classes and methods from the Foundation Framework, making it possible to create any app one can imagine.

Other data types are also inherited in the same fashion. Just have a look at the following table (source – `http://www.rubymotion.com/developer-center/guides/runtime`):

Ruby class	Ancestors
foo	NSObject → Kernel
String	NSMutableString → NSString → Comparable → NSObject → Kernel
Array	NSMutableArray → NSArray → Enumerable → NSObject → Kernel
Hash	NSMutableDictionary → NSDictionary → Enumerable → NSObject → Kernel
Numeric	Comparable → NSNumber → NSValue → NSObject → Kernel
Time	Comparable → NSDate → NSObject → Kernel

You must have noticed that strings created in RubyMotion inherit from `NSMutableString` instead of `NSMutable`. Isn't that strange? It will be good to know the difference between these two. `NSMutableString` objects provide us with methods to change the underlying array of characters that they represent, while `NSString` objects do not. For example, `NSMutableString` provides us methods such as `appendString`, `deleteCharactersInRange`, `insertString`, and `replaceOccurencesWithString`. All these methods operate directly on the `NSMutableString` object in memory, which means we can modify the original value. On the other hand, `NSString` is a create-once-then-read-only string. We have many manipulation methods (`substring`, `uppercaseString`, and so on) for `NSString` objects. However, they return a new `NSString` object and never actually modify the existing string in memory, as shown here:

```
NSString.new.strip!          # raises RuntimeError: can't
  # modify frozen/immutable string

NSMutableString.new.strip!   # works
```

As there is no read-only string in Ruby and we need to update the string too, we are using `NSMutableString` by default. The same goes for arrays and hashes that are inherited from `NSMutableArray` and `NSMutableDictionary` respectively.

Foundation comes with the `NSObject` root object class, as well as a set of other primitive object classes. In RubyMotion, `Object` is an alias of `NSObject`, making `NSObject` the root class of all Ruby classes.

Interfacing with C and Objective-C

Although working with RubyMotion does not require one to learn Objective-C, or even C for that matter, sometimes when you want to use the iOS API, knowledge of its Ruby equivalent is beneficial. Objective-C is a superset of the C language. Objective-C methods can therefore accept and return C-language types.

Types

C language—and indirectly Objective-C—has a set of basic data types that are used in the iOS SDK APIs. In order to accept or return these data types, we need some equivalent data types for Ruby.

For example, let's create a function named `foo` that accepts a C integer type as a parameter and returns the `some_number` integer:

```
int foo(int some_number)
{
  return some_number;
}
```

So, if we want to call the preceding function from Ruby, we will require some equivalent Ruby type. Basic C types cannot be created from Ruby directly, but are automatically converted from and to equivalent Ruby types. You don't have to worry, RubyMotion will take care of this for you.

Let's discuss all of the basic C types and discuss how they are converted from C data types to Ruby data types:

- `void`:
    - From Ruby to C – `nil` is similar to `void`.
    - From C to Ruby – `void` is similar to `nil`.
- `char`, `short`, `int`, `long`, and `long_long`:
    - From Ruby to C – If the object is `Fixnum` or `Bignum`, the value is returned. If the object is `true` or `false`, `1` or `0` are returned respectively. The `char` data type is mapped with `string` and the value returned is the same.
    - From C to Ruby – Either a `Fixnum` or `Bignum` object is returned.
- `Bool/BOOL`:
    - From Ruby to C – If the value of an object is `false` or `nil`, `false` will be returned, else `true` will be returned. Whereas, for `0`, `Fixnum true` will be returned.
    - From C to Ruby – `true` or `false` will be returned.

- `float` and `double`:
  - From Ruby to C:
    - For a `float` object, a value is returned.
    - For `true` or `false`, `1.0` or `0.0` are returned respectively.
    - If the object responds to the `to_f` message, the message is sent and the result is returned.
  - From C to Ruby – it is the `float` object.

Enumerations and constants

Generally, C code uses enumerations and constants extensively, but we don't have these in Ruby. So they are mapped to constants of the `Object` class. Both enumerations and constants defined by the Foundation can be directly accessed.

For example, `NSNotFound` is an enumeration and we can directly access it as shown here:

```
if ary.indexOfObject(obj) == NSNotFound
  # Some Code
end
```

Also, a constant such as `AVMediaTypeAudio` can be directly accessed.

> There are many enumerations or constants defined in the iOS SDK that start with a lowercase letter, such as `kCLLocationAccuracyNearestTenMeters`, which starts with k. But since Ruby constants always begin with a capital letter, their names must be changed by making the lowercase of the first letter uppercase. Therefore, the constant from the preceding example becomes `KCLLocationAccuracyNearestTenMeters;` (starting with a capital K) in Ruby.
>
> ```
> locationManager.desiredAccuracy =
> kCLLocationAccuracyNearestTenMeters;
> # NameError: undefined local variable or method
> locationManager.desiredAccuracy =
> KCLLocationAccuracyNearestTenMeters; # works
> ```

Functions

C functions are available as methods to be used in Ruby code in RubyMotion.

For example, the `CGPointMake` function can be used in Ruby to create a rectangular structure.

```
pt = CGPointMake(100, 200)
''Hello''.drawAtPoint(pt, withFont: font)
```

Many functions in the iOS SDK start with a capital letter. And there is also a possibility that a few of them accept no arguments; in such cases, it can create confusion and the compiler may treat such expressions as constants. So it is very important to use parentheses explicitly when calling such functions, as shown in the following example:

```
NSHomeDirectory    # NameError: uninitialized constant
 # NSHomeDirectory
NSHomeDirectory() # works
```

 Inline functions, which are implemented in the framework's header, are also supported by RubyMotion.

Structures

A structure is a collection of one or more variables, possibly of different data types, grouped together under a single name for convenient handling. To map C structures with Ruby, RubyMotion uses classes, which means structures can be created in Ruby and then passed to APIs that expect C structures. Similarly, APIs returning C structures will return an instance of the appropriate structure class.

A structure class has an `accessor` method for each field of the corresponding C structure it wraps.

For example, the following piece of code creates a `CGPoint` structure, sets its x and y fields, and then passes it to the `drawAtPoint:withFont:` method:

```
pt = CGPoint.new
pt.x = 100
pt.y = 200
''Hello''.drawAtPoint(pt, withFont: font)
```

We can also pass this value directly to the constructor:

```
pt = CGPoint.new(100, 200)
''Hello''.drawAtPoint(pt, withFont: font)
```

RubyMotion will also accept arrays for our convenience. They must contain the same number and type of objects expected in the structure. Here is an example:

```
''Hello''.drawAtPoint([100, 200], withFont: font)
```

Pointers

C and Objective-C both commonly make use of pointers and therefore it is extensively used in the iOS SDK too. In the iOS SDK, pointers are usually used as arguments to return objects by reference. For example, the `NSData` method expects an error pointer that will be set to an `NSError` object in case of a failure.

As there is no pointer concept in Ruby, RubyMotion uses the `Pointer` class in order to create and manipulate pointers. To create a new pointer, use the following syntax:

```
name = Pointer.new(:char)
```

We can see that we have passed `char` in a `new` initializer, which will create a string pointer. Similarly, to create a different type of pointer, we can pass the following parameters in the `Pointer` class (source – `http://www.rubymotion.com/developer-center/guides/runtime/#_pointers`):

C type pointer	Runtime type string	Shortcut symbol
id*	""@""	:object
Char	""c""	:char
unsigned char*	""C""	:uchar
short*	""s""	:short
unsigned short*	""S""	:ushort
int*	""i""	:int
unsigned int*	""I""	:uint
long*	""l""	:long
unsigned long*	""L""	:ulong
long long*	""q""	:long_long
unsigned long long*	""Q""	:ulong_long
float	""f""	:float
double*	""d""	:double

Pointers to C characters, which are also called **C strings**, are automatically converted from and to String objects by RubyMotion.

Classes

Creating a class in Ruby is simple, but since the iOS SDK is written in Objective-C, it is necessary to understand Objective-C interfaces and learn how to use them with Ruby.

An Objective-C interface always starts with a minus or a plus sign, which is used to declare an instance or class method.

For example, the following interface declares the foo instance method on the Foo class:

```
@class Foo
- (id) foo;
@end
```

 The methods that instances of a class can use are called **instance methods** and are marked with a minus sign.

The following declares the foo class method on the same class:

```
@class Foo
+ (id) foo;
@end
```

 The names of the methods that can be used by class objects are preceded by a plus sign.

As seen in the previous section, arguments in Objective-C methods can be named with a keyword. The following interface declares the sharedInstanceWithObject:andObject: class method on the Test class:

```
@class Test
+ (id) sharedInstanceWithObject: (id) obj1 andObject: (id) obj2;
@end
```

The corresponding Ruby method for the preceding code will be as follows:

```
instance = Test.sharedInstanceWithObject(obj1, andObject:obj2)
```

It will call the `sharedInstanceWithObject` method of the `Test` class, where `obj1` and `obj2` are variables of the arguments.

Objective-C messages

We can send and define Objective-C messages using RubyMotion. As Objective-C uses named arguments, which is unlike Ruby methods, it looks different from a typical Ruby method if it contains more than one argument.

Each argument in Objective-C has a keyword associated with it and the final Objective-C message is the combination of all these keywords.

```
UIColor *myColor = [UIColor colorWithRed:0.5f green:0.5f blue:0.5f
alpha:1.0f];
```

Objective-C messages can be sent from RubyMotion using a similar syntax.

```
myColor = UIColor.colorWithRed(0.5, green:0.5, blue:0.5, alpha:1)
```

The message keywords are `colorWithRed:`, `green:`, `blue:`, and `alpha:`.
The complete message is the combination of these keywords. If you are a Ruby developer, you will probably find it strange to see the colon in the Ruby code. The reason is that this is called a **named parameter** and it is very common in RubyMotion applications. As we interact a lot with Objective-C methods and these receive named parameters, we have to pass them in this way.

 The syntax used to define Objective-C selectors was added to RubyMotion and is not part of the Ruby standard.

RubyMotion selectors

The RubyMotion runtime provides convenient shortcuts for certain Objective-C selectors (source – `http://www.rubymotion.com`).

Selector	Shortcut
setFoo:	foo=
isFoo	foo?
objectForKey:	[]
setObject:forKey:	[]=

Memory management

Memory management is an important programming principle of handling the life cycles of objects and releasing them when they are no longer needed in your application. Management of object memory is necessary to have good performance; if an application doesn't free unneeded objects, its memory footprint grows and performance suffers.

RubyMotion provides automatic memory management; you do not need to reclaim unused objects. Also, as memory in any iOS device is limited, the bad acting application would just be killed at some point.

Memory management in a Cocoa application that doesn't use garbage collection is based on a reference-counting method. RubyMotion also uses reference-counting ways to reclaim memory. When you create or copy an object, its retain count is 1. Thereafter, other objects may express an ownership interest in your object, which increments its retain count. The owners of an object may also surrender their possession interest in it, which reduces the retain count. When the retain count becomes zero, the object is deallocated (destroyed).

Objects created by Objective-C or the Core-Foundation-style APIs are automatically managed by RubyMotion. There is no need to send the retain, release, or auto-release messages to them, or to use the `CFRetain` or `CFRelease` functions.

Summary

Let's recap what we have just learned in this chapter:

- How Objective-C and Ruby work together
- How RubyMotion objects are inherited from Objective-C
- How RubyMotion interfaces with C and Objective-C
- Memory management offered with RubyMotion

In the next chapter, we will learn how we can use the **Model-View-Controller** (**MVC**) design principle in our RubyMotion application. We will discuss in detail about the MVC architecture. Later in the chapter, we will have some hands-on examples to learn how to integrate our mobile application with an external API.

4
Mastering MVC Paradigm

"Model-View-Controller is not an inescapable law of purity, but a pragmatic principle of effectiveness."

—Anonymous

In this chapter we will learn about Model-View-Controller, popularly abbreviated as MVC, which is a design principle based on the ideas of code reusability and **separation of concerns** (**SoC**). This architecture imposes serious constraints on the structure of an application, however, surprisingly these restrictions make it considerably easier to design and maintain the application. In this chapter we will be covering the following topics:

- Understanding the Model-View-Controller paradigm
- Creating a RubyMotion application using MVC
- Connecting to an external API
- Enhancing the application with search and images
- The do-it-yourself exercise

Model-View-Controller (MVC)

Model-View-Controller (**MVC**) is a design principle that separates the representation of information from the user's interaction. The main purpose of MVC is to make the code more modular and reusable, which increases the product quality.

Most of the popular commercial and noncommercial application frameworks are created to enforce the MVC design pattern. However, RubyMotion does not force you to use MVC style, but this way of programming is central to a good design for application development. If we make use of MVC while developing our application, it will be beneficial for us later on, as we will be able to add new features more easily.

 Apple's Cocoa framework is also based on Model-View-Controller.

As the name implies, the application is divided into three distinct parts: model, view, and controller, where model encapsulates application data, view displays and allows editing the data, and controller is the place where logic of the interaction between the two (model and view) resides. Let's understand each of them individually.

Model

The model contains the application data and business rules. The model could just be the actual data store, either in-memory (maybe as an `NSArray` or `NSDictionary` class) or to-and-from disk. In a more complex app, you may choose to use a SQLite database or Core Data, and your model would be a simple instance or one piece of data.

View

A view is that part of an application that outputs information from the model via the controller. The logic should never be written in the view; the sole purpose of the view is only to present information. In iOS, and also in RubyMotion, most views are subclasses of the `UIView` class that provide the capability for handling touch events and drawings. The `UIKit` framework contains classes to draw typical interface elements such as tables (lists), buttons, text fields, and sliders.

Controller

A controller is a link between the model and view. A controller acts as an intermediary between one or more application views, and one or more of its models. In iOS, the controller is generally a subclass of `UIViewController` that also manages a view; this class is also responsible for responding to delegation messages and target-action messages.

The Model-View-Controller layers are very closely coupled, as shown in the following diagram:

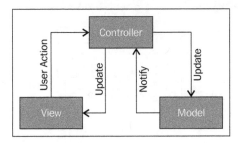

The **View** and **Controller** layers interact through **User Action** and **Update** as shown in the diagram. Whenever the **View** layer creates or modifies data, it is communicated to **Controller** through **User Action**. Similarly, whenever **Model** updates any change it will first **Notify** the **Controller** and will then be reflected on the **View** by an **Update**.

The restaurant application

Now to better understand MVC we will create a `restro` application. This application will search restaurants in a city. Does the world need another restaurant application? No, but that won't stop us from writing one. On a serious note, it will help us to explore many features of RubyMotion and will also help us learn and master MVC.

Let's understand what we are going to do in this application. A restaurant application will list out the eat outs, which we can search based on the city. The list of places will have a thumbnail image along with information related to the restaurant.

It's good practice to imagine views of your application in the form of a mockup. The best way to do this is by using a white board with illustrations that you envision for your application.

You must be wondering where all this data will come from. Do I need to hardcode it right into my application? That does not make sense! To begin with, we will hardcode the values; but later on, as we proceed and evolve, we will learn how to use an external API to fetch information, which is something often done in real-world applications. We have created a backend API exclusively for this book, having all the data available for practice.

Let's now create a `restro` project with RubyMotion, using the magical `motion` command:

```
>motion create restro
    Create restro
    Create restro/.gitignore
    Create restro/Rakefile
    Create restro/app
    Create restro/app/app_delegate.rb
    Create restro/resources
    Create restro/spec
    Create restro/spec/main_spec.rb
```

As discussed in earlier chapters, the `motion` command will create the basic structure for a RubyMotion project.

> Feel free to choose your IDE. If you are using RubyMine, you can also create and run the application from the IDE.

Creating a model

For our `restro` application, let's brainstorm what entities and attributes will be required. The first thing that comes to mind is a restaurant entity having the following attributes:

- `name`: This will contain the name of the application
- `thumb_url_image`: This will contain the image URL for the restaurant
- `food_type`: This will contain the type of food the restaurant serves
- `desc`: This will contain a small description about the restaurant

Looks good! Let's create a model, `Restaurant`, that will store all the information related to restaurants.

Create a ruby (`.rb`) file, which will be our model inside the `app` folder, and name it `restaurant.rb`:

```ruby
class Restaurant
attr_accessor :name,:thumb_url_image, :food_type, :desc
  def initialize(restaurant)
    @name =restaurant['name']
    @thumb_url_image = restaurant['thumb_url_image']
    @food_type = restaurant['food_type']
    @desc = restaurant['desc']
  end
end
```

We have created a class called `Restaurant`. Generally we need to first create getter and setter methods for the variables. However, in Ruby we don't need to separately create getters and setters, instead we use a single method called `attr_accessor` to do that; this idea of syntactic sugar is commonly used in various trivial jobs in Ruby, which indeed saves a lot of time.

 Syntactic sugar is a syntax within a programming language that is designed to make things easier to read or express. An example of syntactic sugar is as follows:

```ruby
attr_accessor :name,:thumb_url_image, :food_type, :desc
```

After setting up `attr_accessor`, in order to assign values while creating an object of the `Restaurant` class, we have created an `initialize` method. This gives us a chance to write code that sets up our object's state.

```
def initialize(restaurant)
  @name =restaurant['name']
  @thumb_url_image = restaurant['thumb_url_image']
  @food_type = restaurant['food_type']
  @desc = restaurant['desc']
end
```

Whenever we create an object of the `Restaurant` class, it will call the `name` method, and initialize and execute it. We have to pass a hash of restaurants while creating the object. To test the model, let's fire up our terminal in the `application` directory and run `rake`:

```
>restaurant = Restaurant.new({'name'=> "Pizza madness", 'thumb_url_
image'=> nil, 'food_type'=>"italian", 'desc'=>"Pizza at your door step in
30 min"})
=> #<Restaurant:0xb5376a0 @name="Pizza madness" @thumb_url_image=nil @
food_type="italian" @desc="Pizza at your door step in 30 min">

> restaurant.name
=> "Pizza madness"
```

Great! Our `Restaurant` class is created and we can now create objects of this class.

Writing more code

A lot of iOS applications use table structure to represent their information. This method of design is best for information-based applications, like the one we have in our example. So let's create a table view for our landing page, which will populate a list of restaurants.

Let's now update the `app_delegate.rb` file inside the `app` folder:

```
class AppDelegate
  def application(application,
                 didFinishLaunchingWithOptions:launchOptions)
    @window = UIWindow.alloc.initWithFrame
      (UIScreen.mainScreen.applicationFrame)
    @window.rootViewController =
      RestroController.alloc.initWithStyle(UITableViewStylePlain)
    @window.rootViewController.wantsFullScreenLayout = true
    @window.makeKeyAndVisible
    true
  end
end
```

The `UIWindow` class defines an object known as `window`, which manages and coordinates different views of your application, and displays them on the device screen. A `UIScreen` object contains the bounding rectangle of the device's entire screen. So `UIScreen.mainScreen.applicationFrame` returns the rectangle size according to the screen size and orientation of the device. Also we need to tell the `UIWindow` object which controller to load:

```
@window.rootViewController =
    RestroController.alloc.initWithStyle(UITableViewStylePlain)
```

We have assigned the `RestroController` class as the root controller for our application in `AppDelegate`. So let's create `restro_controller.rb` in the `app` folder:

```
class RestroController < UITableViewController
  def viewDidLoad
    super
    @restaurant1 = Restaurant.new({'name'=> "Pizza madness",
        'thumb_url_image'=> nil, 'food_type'=>"italian",
            'desc'=>"Pizza at your door step in 30 min"})
    @restaurant2 = Restaurant.new({'name'=> "Lavasa",
        'thumb_url_image' => nil,'food_type'=>"italian",
            'desc'=>"best Coffee house in town"})
    @restaurants = [@restaurant1,@restaurant2]
    view.backgroundColor = UIColor.whiteColor
    @myTableView = UITableView.alloc.initWithFrame
        (view.bounds, style:UITableViewStylePlain)
    @myTableView.dataSource = self
    @myTableView.delegate = self
    view.addSubview(@myTableView)
  end

  def tableView(tableView, numberOfRowsInSection:section)
    @restaurants.count
  end

  def tableView(tableView, cellForRowAtIndexPath:indexPath)

    @reuseIdentifier ||= "CELL_IDENTIFIER"

    cell = tableView.dequeueReusableCellWithIdentifier
        (@reuseIdentifier) || begin
        UITableViewCell.alloc.initWithStyle
            (UITableViewCellStyleDefault, reuseIdentifier:@
reuseIdentifier)
    end
    cell.textLabel.text = @restaurants[indexPath.row].name
    cell
  end

end
```

Now let's fire up our terminal again and see what we have done:

```
>rake
```

The previous screenshot shows a table structure with a list of restaurants. Now that's some impressive work. Let's now understand what we did in the previous section. Our code has three parts — model, view, and controller. We have already explained about the restaurant model. We first created an object for the model and assigned some value to it:

```
@restaurant1 = Restaurant.new({
    'name'=> "Pizza madness", 'thumb_url_image'=> nil,
    'food_type'=>"italian",
    'desc'=>"Pizza at your door step in 30 min"})

@restaurant2 = Restaurant.new({
    'name'=> "Lavasa",
    'thumb_url_image' => nil,
    'food_type'=>"italian",
    'desc'=>"best Coffee house in town"})
```

We have created two objects and passed a hash to them, as we have explained in the previous section. The remaining code has two parts, a controller and a view; let's understand them one by one.

Restaurant controller

In the previous example, the Restaurant controller inherits from UITableViewController, which is a subclass of UIViewController. The UIViewController class provides the fundamental view-management model for your apps.

We rarely instantiate the UIViewController objects directly. Instead, it is generally instantiated via a class that is a subclass of the UIViewController class, as we did in the previous example. It manages a set of views that make up a portion of your app's user interface. The most important thing in an iOS controller is its lifecycle. There are various actions that are called at different phases of the application. The lifecycle includes actions such as Initialize, ViewDidLoad, ViewWillAppear, ViewDidAppear, ViewWillDisappear, ViewDidDisappear, ViewDidUnload, and Dispose. So these events are called automatically and dynamically. Whenever we create an object of the controller it calls Initialize, before loading the view for the controller, ViewDidLoad will be called. The complete lifecycle of a controller can be seen in the following diagram:

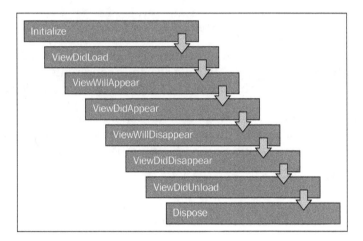

 viewDidUnload and viewWillUnload are deprecated in iOS 6.0.

You can see in our restro controller that we have written a lot of logic in `ViewDidLoad`, so all the code written in this block will execute before the loading of the view.

 It's important to note that these methods are attached to `UIViewController` and not to `UIViews`.

Restaurant view

The `UITableView` class is used to create one of the most common types of views used in iOS applications, that is, the table view. We can see only one column in our application. This is because the `UITableView` instance is limited to a single column as it is designed for a device with a small screen. `UITableView` is a subclass of `UIScrollView`, which allows users to scroll through the table, although `UITableView` allows vertical scrolling only.

Table views can have one of two styles, `UITableViewStylePlain` (for example, iOS contacts) or `UITableViewStyleGrouped` (for example, iOS settings). When you create a `UITableView` instance, you must specify the table style; this style cannot be changed. For our application, since we do not require to group the restaurants we will use `UITableViewStylePlain`.

```
@myTableView = UITableView.alloc.initWithFrame
    (view.bounds, style:UITableViewStylePlain)
```

A view is bound to return `CGRect` with an empty origin point. The `CGRect` class is very commonly used in iOS apps. Its data structure represents the location and dimensions of a rectangle, which is used to set the size of the table view.

The `UITableView` class provides a lot of options, but it needs to know what data we are trying to show and what to do when the user interacts with that data. This is where the `datasource` and `delegate` properties come in:

```
@myTableView.dataSource = self
@myTableView.delegate = self
```

We have to return the number of rows to be created using `numberOfRowsInSection`:

```
def tableView(tableView, numberOfRowsInSection:section)
  @restaurants.count
end
```

The `tableView:numberOfRowsInSection` property tells the `UITableview` datasource to return the number of rows in a given section of a table view. So in our example, the number of rows will be equal to the total restaurant count.

Moving forward, let's understand `UITableViewCell`, which is the subclass of `UIView`; using this class our rows are displayed in table form. To access the contents of the cell, we have properties, such as `textLabel` and `imageView`, to use them for setting their attributes such as text color, font, image, and highlighted image. You can also easily give a custom look to tables by using different iOS methods. Another property `cellForRowAtIndexPath` either creates a new cell or recycles an offscreen one and populates it with the data corresponding to `indexPath`, and returns the cell. The following code snippet shows how a more complete implementation looks:

```
def tableView(tableView, cellForRowAtIndexPath:indexPath)

  @reuseIdentifier ||= "CELL_IDENTIFIER"

  cell = tableView.dequeueReusableCellWithIdentifier(@
reuseIdentifier) || begin
      UITableViewCell.alloc.initWithStyle(UITableViewCellStyleDefault,
reuseIdentifier:@reuseIdentifier)
    end
    cell.textLabel.text = @restaurants[indexPath.row].name
    cell
  end
```

The `UITableView` class only displays enough data to fill the iPhone screen—it does not really matter how much data you might have in total. The `UITableView` class does this by reusing cells that scrolled off the screen. When cells scroll off the screen (either the top or the bottom) the table view will queue up cells that are no longer needed. When it asks the datasource for the cell of a particular row, you can check that queue of cells to see if there are any available for use:

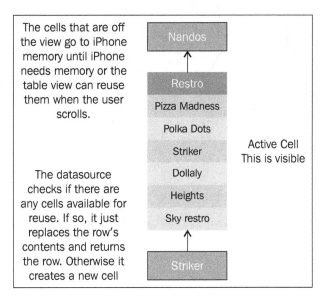

The whole point of dequeueReusableCell is that the process of creating a new view hierarchy for UITableViewCell is rather expensive. If you recreated the cell each time you needed it, the scrolling behavior wouldn't be as nice as it is.

With dequeueReusableCellWithIdentifier for tableView, you can greatly speed things up. Instead of instantiating a lot of cells, you can just instantiate the ones that are needed, which means only those cells that are visible (this is handled automatically). When scrolling to an area in the list for which the cells are not yet visually represented, instead of instantiating new ones, you can reuse the already existing ones.

```
cell = tableView.dequeueReusableCellWithIdentifier
    (@reuseIdentifier) || begin
        UITableViewCell.alloc.initWithStyle
            (UITableViewCellStyleDefault, reuseIdentifier:@
reuseIdentifier)
    end
```

Next we have assigned a display value for each row in the following way:

```
cell.textLabel.text = @restaurants[indexPath.row].name
```

 In Ruby, *a* || = *b* means if *a* is nil/false, assign it the value of *b*.

Connecting to an external API

Right now we have hardcoded the object values, which usually never happens in a real-world application; let's get these values from an external API. For practicing purposes we have created an external API to get the data in JSON format.

If you visit http://restro.nalwaya.com/restaurants/search. json?city=Chicago or use the curl command instead, it will return the restaurants we have seeded for Chicago in JSON format (note that this is fictitious data, you might not actually find them in Chicago city).

Let's run the following curl command to get the data:

```
> curl "http://restro.nalwaya.com/restaurants/search.json?city=Chicago"
[{
  "name":"Polka Dots",
    "thumb_url_image":"http://restro.nalwaya.com/system/
```

```
    restaurants/avatars/000/000/001/thumb/hotel.jpg?1352812187",
  "food_type":"Italian",
  "desc":"Best Italian food in city"
},
{
  "name":"Striker",
    "thumb_url_image":"http://restro.nalwaya.com/system/
    restaurants/avatars/000/000/002/thumb/
    20121111_135450.jpg?1353424527",
  "food_type":"Italian",
  "desc":"Best food in the town"
},
{
  "name":"Pizza madness",
    thumb_url_image":"http://restro.nalwaya.com/system/
    restaurants/avatars/000/000/003/thumb/
    restaurant-icon-96da9e9f58682c8035c4fa4ee04bdcca.gif?1353425778",
  "food_type": "Pizza Mania",
  "desc":"Pizza in 30 min"},
{
  "name":"Dollaly",
    "thumb_url_image":"http://restro.nalwaya.com/system/
    restaurants/avatars/000/000/004/thumb/
    restaurant_table3.jpg?1353425829", "food_type":"Indian",
  "desc":"Best beer in town"
}]
```

 curl is a command-line tool for transferring data using various protocols.

Now we will show the list of restaurants in Chicago city, which we are getting from our source in our restro application. Since we are getting data in JSON format, we need to convert this JSON object to a Ruby object.

Create a file by the name json_parser.rb in the app folder:

```
class JSONParser
  def self.parse_from_url(url)
    data = DataParser.parse(url)

    error_ptr = Pointer.new(:object)
```

```
      json = NSJSONSerialization.JSONObjectWithData(data, options:0,
  error:error_ptr)
      unless json
        alert = UIAlertView.new··
        alert.message = error_ptr[0]
        alert.show
      end
      json
    end
  end
```

The NSJSONSerialization class converts JSON to Foundation objects and converts Foundation objects to JSON.

 RubyMotion has the Pointer class in order to create and manipulate pointers. The type of pointer to create must be provided in the new constructor. So Pointer.new(:object) will create a new pointer with the object class.

We need to fetch the JSON object by sending a request to the server; for that we will create a DataParser class.

Let's create a file by the name data_parser.rb in the app folder:

```
class DataParser
  def self.parse(url)
    error_ptr = Pointer.new(:object)
    data = NSData.alloc.initWithContentsOfURL(NSURL.
URLWithString(url), options:NSDataReadingUncached, error:error_ptr)
    unless data
      alert = UIAlertView.new··
      alert.message = error_ptr[0]
      alert.show

    end
    data
  end
end
```

We will fetch data using the NSUrl class that will pass this data to NSData. NSData and its mutable subclass NSMutableData provides the data objects with an object-oriented wrapping for byte buffers.

Now let's refactor the logic in `restro_controller.rb`, which will fetch data from the API instead of the hardcoded `Restaurant` object we had created in the previous section.

Update the `viewDidLoad` section of `restro_controller.rb`:

```
url = "http://restro.nalwaya.com/restaurants/
      search.json?city=Chicago"
    json = nil
    begin
      json = JSONParser.parse_from_url(url)
    rescue RuntimeError => e
      presentError e.message
    end

    @restaurants = []
    json.each do |restaurant|
      @restaurants << Restaurant.new(restaurant)
    end


    view.backgroundColor = UIColor.whiteColor
    @myTableView = UITableView.alloc.initWithFrame(view.bounds,
  style:UITableViewStylePlain)
    @myTableView.dataSource = self
    @myTableView.delegate = self
    view.addSubview(@myTableView)
```

In case of an error, let's face it gracefully by displaying the error message using a pop-up. So let's create a `presentError` method in `restaurant_controller.rb`, and print the error on pop-up:

```
def presentError error_msg
  alert = UIAlertView.new··
  alert.message = error_msg
  alert.show·

end
```

Go to the terminal and start the application with the `rake` command.

We can see that the list of restaurants is shown dynamically from the JSON API.

Search restaurant by city

In the previous section we were only showing restaurants in Chicago. If you noticed, it was hardcoded in the URL itself and was not generic. In this section we will make the application more generic and allow the user to search data based on a parameter city.

Update `restro_controller.rb` as follows:

```
class RestroController < UITableViewController
  def viewDidLoad
    super
    @restaurants = []
    searchBar = UISearchBar.alloc.initWithFrame(CGRectMake(0, 0, self.
tableView.frame.size.width, 0))
    searchBar.delegate = self;
    searchBar.showsCancelButton = true;
    searchBar.sizeToFit
```

```ruby
    view.tableHeaderView = searchBar
    view.dataSource = view.delegate = self
    searchBar.text = 'Chicago'

    searchBarSearchButtonClicked(searchBar)

  end
  def searchBarSearchButtonClicked(searchBar)
    query = searchBar.text.stringByAddingPercentEscapesUsingEncoding(N
SUTF8StringEncoding)
    url = "http://restro.nalwaya.com/restaurants/search.
json?city=#{query}"
    @restaurants.clear
    json = nil
    begin
      json = JSONParser.parse_from_url(url)
    rescue RuntimeError => e
      presentError e.message
    end

    @restaurants = []
    json.each do |restaurant|
      @restaurants << Restaurant.new(restaurant)
    end

    view.reloadData
    searchBar.resignFirstResponder
  end
  def searchBarCancelButtonClicked(searchBar)
    searchBar.resignFirstResponder
  end
  def tableView(tableView, numberOfRowsInSection:section)
    @restaurants.count
  end

  def tableView(tableView, cellForRowAtIndexPath:indexPath)
    @reuseIdentifier ||= "CELL_IDENTIFIER"
    cell = tableView.dequeueReusableCellWithIdentifier(@
reuseIdentifier) || begin
      UITableViewCell.alloc.initWithStyle(UITableViewCellStyleDefault,
reuseIdentifier:@reuseIdentifier)
    end
```

```
      cell.textLabel.text = @restaurants[indexPath.row].name
      cell
    end
  end
end
```

Start the simulator by the `rake` command, and you can see that your toolbar is replaced with a search box with the default value **Chicago**.

What just happened

The `UISearchBar` class implements a text field control for text-based searches. The `UISearchBar` object does not actually perform any search; it is just a view, which we can see on the device. To make the search work, we use a delegate, which is an object conforming to the `UISearchBarDelegate` protocol, to implement the actions when text is entered and buttons are clicked. The `UISearchBarDelegate` protocol defines the optional methods you implement to make a `UISearchBar` control functional.

The UISearchBar object provides the user interface for a search field on a bar, but it's the application's responsibility to implement the actions when buttons are tapped. We can implement this using various methods available, which are explained next.

The methods used for editing text are as follows:

- searchBar:textDidChange: This tells the delegate that the user changed the search text
- searchBar:shouldChangeTextInRange:replacementText: This asks the delegate if text in a specified range should be replaced with the given text
- searchBarShouldBeginEditing: This asks the delegate if editing should begin in the specified search bar
- searchBarTextDidBeginEditing: This tells the delegate when the user begins editing the search text
- searchBarShouldEndEditing: This asks the delegate if editing should stop in the specified search bar
- searchBarTextDidEndEditing: This tells the delegate that the user finished editing the search text

The methods used for different click events on various buttons in the search bar are as follows:

- searchBarBookmarkButtonClicked: This tells the delegate that the bookmark button was tapped
- searchBarCancelButtonClicked: This tells the delegate that the cancel button was tapped
- searchBarSearchButtonClicked: This tells the delegate that the search results list button was tapped
- searchBarResultsListButtonClicked: This tells the delegate that the search button was tapped

The method used for the scope button is as follows:

- searchBar:selectedScopeButtonIndexDidChange: This tells the delegate that the scope button selection changed

 As a minimum, the delegate needs to perform the actual search when the text is entered in the text field.

We have implemented searchBarSearchButtonClicked(searchBar),
and whenever the search button is clicked this action will be called:

```
def searchBarSearchButtonClicked(searchBar)
    query = searchBar.text.stringByAddingPercentEscapesUsingEncoding(N
SUTF8StringEncoding)
    url = "http://restro.nalwaya.com/restaurants/search.
json?city=#{query}"
    @restaurants.clear
    json = nil
    begin
      json = JSONParser.parse_from_url(url)
    rescue RuntimeError => e
      presentError e.message
    end

    @restaurants = []
    json.each do |restaurant|
      @restaurants << Restaurant.new(restaurant)
    end

    view.reloadData
    searchBar.resignFirstResponder
  end
```

So, all the results that we have fetched from our web service are stored in the json
variable. We will loop through this object and store the information in our restaurant
model, which we have created in the previous section.

We have to reload the view once we complete the entire task, and this can be done by
using the view.reloadData class.

Picture speaks louder than words

Let's now show a thumbnail image of a restaurant next to its name. In the JSON API
call, we also see that we are getting the link for the restaurant image. So, we use this
URL to display the image with the restaurant name in the table view.

Update `restaurant_controller.rb` as follows:

```
def tableView(tableView, cellForRowAtIndexPath:indexPath)

  @reuseIdentifier ||= "CELL_IDENTIFIER"

  cell = tableView.dequeueReusableCellWithIdentifier(@
reuseIdentifier) || begin
    UITableViewCell.alloc.initWithStyle(UITableViewCellStyleDefault,
reuseIdentifier:@reuseIdentifier)
  end
  cell.textLabel.text = @restaurants[indexPath.row].name
  cell.imageView.image = UIImage.alloc.initWithData(NSData.alloc.
initWithContentsOfURL(NSURL.URLWithString(@restaurants[indexPath.row].
thumb_url_image)))
  cell
end
```

`UIImage.alloc.initWithData` initializes and returns the image object with the specified data, and `NSData.alloc.initWithContentsOfURL` initializes a newly allocated data object initialized with the data from the location specified by a URL.

Once again let's fire up our simulator to see the progress. Run `rake` from the `app` folder.

Isn't that simple! We can now see an image displayed next to the restaurant name.

Play time

It's time for a small do-it-yourself exercise. In the same application put some description about the restaurant in each row of the table.

We get the description in our API and it is already stored in the `Restaurant` object. To display this in the view you can use `detailTextLabel` on the cell object, as we have used in `textLabel`.

Summary

Let's recap what we have learned in this iteration:

- Model-View-Controller architecture
- Using an MVC design with RubyMotion
- Connecting our application with an external API
- Augmenting our app with search and images

In the next chapter, we will turn our attention to user interface (UI) for mobile applications. UI is a key area in mobile application development, and we will learn about various Objective-C classes, which make user interface more interactive, and how they can be used in our RubyMotion application.

5

User Interface – Cosmetics for Your App

"Design is not just what it looks like and feels like. Design is how it works."

- Steve Jobs

The ultimate objective of a user interface design is to make a user's interaction with the application a simple and pleasant experience. It is important to understand the basic elements of a technology to make a friendly user interface for end users. In this chapter, we will learn about the different elements required to craft a user interface for iOS applications with RubyMotion. Apps running on iOS-based devices have a limited amount of screen space for exposing content. This is the most expensive real estate for any iOS developer, and we must be creative enough to devise ways to present information to the user and make use of this precious space economically.

You can always customize your user interface to create a stunning look for your application. But as you design the user interface of your application, there are some preferred ways, such as the placement of a few controls, that can be adopted to give users an amicable environment similar to that of built-in apps. As you know, there is no dedicated hardware for a back button on the iPhone; we must always make sure to keep one on the upper-left corner before the user gets lost while navigating from one page to another. A good way to achieve this is by using a typical iOS navigation bar that is provided in the iOS SDK. The benefit of using such conventional UI elements is that they act gracefully at the time of updates, when Apple introduces a redesign of these elements. Completely custom-made elements do not receive updates. When you use these standard APIs, you can still customize the appearance for most of the UI elements and still receive automatic updates.

In the iOS SDK, the `UIKit` framework provides a wide range of UI elements that you can use in your app. In this chapter, we will cover the following topics in detail:

- Bars
- Basic UI elements
- The Restaurant app—let's make it pretty

Bars

There are many types of bars available in the iOS SDK, such as a tab bar, navigation bar, toolbar, and status bar. These are UI elements that have been designed with explicit behavior and appearance. Although having bars is not mandatory in your application, it's advisable to add them as they make life easier for both developers and users alike. These bars provide common anchors to users of iOS devices who are familiar with the information they provide and the function they perform.

In this section, we will discuss the following types of bars in detail:

- The tab bar
- The navigation bar and toolbar
- The status bar

The tab bar

A tab bar gives people the ability to switch between different subtasks, views, or modes. A tab bar is placed at the bottom of the screen, mainly at the footer section, which we can see in most of the popular iOS applications. Each tab in a tab bar has a separate view that can be used to initiate the navigation between your app's different modes, and it can also convey information about the state of each mode.

On the iPhone, a tab bar can display no more than five tabs at a given point in time. If the app has more tabs, the tab bar displays four of them and adds the **More** tab that reveals the additional tabs in a list. On the iPad, a tab bar can display more than five tabs.

 The size of a tab bar image is typically 30 x 30 px. If this image is too large to fit on the tab bar, it is clipped to fit the available size.

First, we'll create some views to understand out topic better:

1. Let's create a sample application to understand this topic more clearly:

```
motion create UserInterfaceApplication

      Create UserInterfaceApplication
      Create UserInterfaceApplication/.gitignore
      Create UserInterfaceApplication/Rakefile
      Create UserInterfaceApplication/app
      Create UserInterfaceApplication/app/app_delegate.rb
      Create UserInterfaceApplication/resources
      Create UserInterfaceApplication/spec
      Create UserInterfaceApplication/spec/main_spec.rb
```

2. Create a file named `tab1_controller.rb` in the `app` folder and add the following code:

```
class Tab1Controller < UIViewController
  def viewDidLoad
      view.backgroundColor = UIColor.
scrollViewTexturedBackgroundColor
    end
end
```

   In the preceding code, we are setting the background color for the view to a custom color that is provided by iOS and is called `scrollViewTexturedBackgroundColor`. This custom color is available with the `UIColor` class. Similarly, we will create two more tabs.

3. Create a file named `tab2_controller.rb` inside the `app` folder and add the following code:

```
class Tab2Controller < UIViewController
    def viewDidLoad
      view.backgroundColor = UIColor.redColor
   end
end
```

4. Create another file named `tab3_controller.rb` inside the `app` folder and add the following code:

```
class Tab3Controller < UIViewController
    def viewDidLoad
       view.backgroundColor = UIColor.whiteColor
    end
end
```

We have created three views with different background colors so that when we switch from one view to another, we can see the difference. Now let's create a tab bar and link it with the three view controllers that we just created.

For this, we can just add the following code in `app_delegate.rb` inside the app folder:

```
class AppDelegate
  def application(application, didFinishLaunchingWithOptions:launchOp
tions)
        @window = UIWindow.alloc.initWithFrame(UIScreen.mainScreen.
bounds)
        @window.rootViewController = createTabBar
        @window.makeKeyAndVisible

    true
  end

  def createTabBar

    tab_bar_controller = UITabBarController.alloc.init
    tab_bar_controller.viewControllers = [
      Tab1Controller.alloc.init,
      Tab2Controller.alloc.init,
      Tab3Controller.alloc.init
    ]
    tab_bar_controller
  end
end
```

In the preceding code, we created a method called `createTabBar` in which we are building a tab bar. A `UITabBarController` class needs an array of `UIViewControllers`. Each element in this array will become a tab on the screen. The three views, which were created earlier, are linked to the tabs of the tab bar respectively. Let's fire up the terminal and see our newly created tab bar:

$rake

This is what we get as our output:

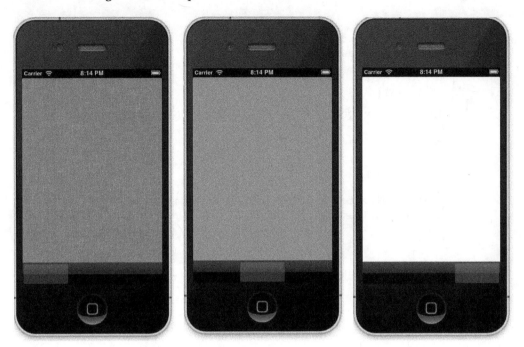

Great! We can see a tab bar at the bottom of the screen with three tabs, and each tab has a view with different background colors.

 UITabBar, which is at the bottom of the screen, has a height of 44 pixels.

Customizing the tab bar

You will always have to label your tabs in the tab bar with a title or an image-like icon. Let's give some titles to our tabs, which we have created in the previous section, and provide some images for them:

1. Update the `tab1_controller.rb` file inside the `app` folder with the following code:

```
class Tab1Controller < UIViewController
  def init

    super
    self.title = "Tab 1"
    self.tabBarItem.image = UIImage.imageNamed('FirstTab.png')
    self
```

```
    end

    def viewDidLoad
        view.backgroundColor = UIColor.
    scrollViewTexturedBackgroundColor
    end
end
```

2. Add the following method in the `tab2_controller.rb` file inside the app folder:

```
def init
    super

    self.tabBarItem = UITabBarItem.alloc.initWithTabBarSystemItem
(UITabBarSystemItemSearch, tag: 1)
    self
end
```

3. Similarly, add the following method in the `tab3_controller.rb` file inside the app folder:

```
def init
    super

    self.tabBarItem = UITabBarItem.alloc.initWithTabBarSystemItem
(UITabBarSystemItemTopRated, tag: 1)
    self
end
```

4. Now, let's test the changes in the iOS simulator:

    $rake

5. Here is what we get:

The result, as you can see, is a tab bar with icons and titles. The UITabBarItem class is responsible for implementing any items or images on the tab bar. By default, it will place any image that you passed with a blue gradient, discarding the color information of the image and using the alpha channel (transparency) information to know where to apply the gradient. A tab bar will always operate in radio mode; this means only one item can be selected at a time.

If you want to display a custom image when a tab is selected, you can do so by using the following code:

```
tab_bar_item.setFinishedSelectedImage(UIImage.
imageNamed("selectedImage"), withFinishedUnselectedImag
e:UIImage.imageNamed("UnselectedImage"))
```

There are two ways to add icons to tabs in the tab bar. Depending on your requirement, you can either add a custom icon or use the common icons provided by Apple. Let's briefly discuss both these ways:

- **Custom icon**: You can design your image and put it in each tab. There is an image property in `tabBarItem` that accepts an image:

```
self.tabBarItem.image = UIImage.imageNamed('FirstTab.png')
```

If your image is in PNG format, you can skip the extension while mentioning the filename, shown as follows:

```
self.tabBarItem.image = UIImage.
imageNamed('FirstTab')
```

- **Common icons provided by iOS**: The following are some common icons provided by the Cocoa library. These will be used directly in our application:

Constant name	Icon
UITabBarSystemItemMore	•••
UITabBarSystemItemFavorites	★
UITabBarSystemItemFeatured	✖
UITabBarSystemItemRecents	🕐
UITabBarSystemItemContacts	👤
UITabBarSystemItemBookmarks	📖
UITabBarSystemItemSearch	🔍
UITabBarSystemItemDownloads	⬇
UITabBarSystemItemMostRecent	⊞
UITabBarSystemItemMostViewed	👥

If you want to change the background of the tab bar to customize an image, use the following code:

```
tab_bar_controller.tabBar.backgroundImage = UIImage.
imageNamed "bgTabBar"
```

The navigation bar

A navigation bar allows navigation through different screens. A navigation bar and a toolbar can be seen at the top of the app screen, just below the status bar. The navigation bar provides a drill-down interface for hierarchical content. You can also provide items for the toolbar that are managed by navigation controllers such as buttons. Let's see how we can create a navigation bar in our app:

1. Update the `app_delegate.rb` file inside the `app` folder with the following code:

```
def createTabBar

    tab_bar_controller = UITabBarController.alloc.init
    tab_bar_controller.viewControllers = [
        UINavigationController.alloc.initWithRootViewController(Tab
1Controller.alloc.init),
        Tab2Controller.alloc.init,
        Tab3Controller.alloc.init
    ]
    tab_bar_controller
  end
```

   In the preceding code, we initialized `Tab1Controller` while initializing `UINavigationController`. In this way, we can generate a navigation bar:

```
UINavigationController.alloc.initWithRootViewController(Tab1Contro
ller.alloc.init)
```

2. Let's fire up the terminal and execute the following command:

   $rake

3. The following is what we get when we execute the command:

That's really cool! We can see a navigation bar appear at the top of the screen. But right now it does nothing. Let's modify the bar and add buttons to it.

 A navigation bar automatically shows some default title text.

Customizing the navigation bar

Now let's customize the navigation bar with a translucent color and add a button to it:

1. Update the `tab1_controller.rb` file inside the `app` folder with the following code:

```
class Tab1Controller < UIViewController
  def init
    super
    self.title = "Tab 1"
```

```
      self.tabBarItem.image = UIImage.imageNamed('FirstTab.png')
      self
   end
   def viewDidLoad
      view.backgroundColor = UIColor.
scrollViewTexturedBackgroundColor

      setupNavigationBar

   end
   def setupNavigationBar

      self.navigationController.navigationBar.barStyle =
UIBarStyleBlackTranslucent;
      right_button_item = UIBarButtonItem.alloc.initWithTitle
('Add',style:UIBarButtonItemStyleBordered,target: self, action:
"click_add"  )
      self.navigationItem.setRightBarButtonItem(right_button_
item)

   end


  def click_add
    @alert_box = UIAlertView.alloc.initWithTitle("Add button
popup",
            message:"You have pressed the 'Add' button",
            delegate: nil,
            cancelButtonTitle: "ok",
            otherButtonTitles:nil)
    @alert_box.show
  end

end
```

2. Let's fire up the terminal and execute the following command:

   `$rake`

3. Here is the output:

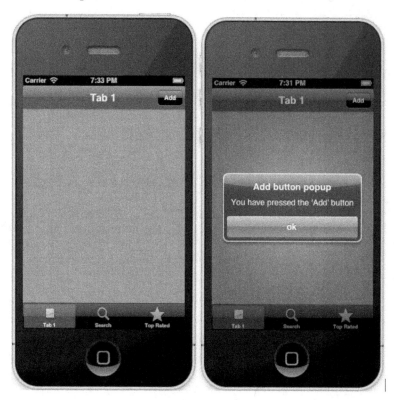

We can see that the navigation toolbar controller is now translucent, and we have an **Add** button in the upper-left corner. When we press the **Add** button, an alert pop-up will appear with the message: **You have pressed the 'Add' button**.

The `UIBarButtonItem` class creates a button, and for each button we have to define an action that will be called when that button is clicked. In our example, we have created the `click_add` action for the `Add` button:

```
UIBarButtonItem.alloc.initWithTitle('Add',style:UIBarButtonItemStyleBo
rdered,target: self, action: "click_add"   )
```

In the preceding code snippet, we created a button with the title set as `Add`. To define the action that has to be performed when the button is clicked, we use the `action` parameter.

Next, we will assign the location of the button on the navigation bar:

```
self.navigationItem.setRightBarButtonItem(right_button_item)
```

Doing this will place a button on the right-hand side of the navigation bar.

 To add a button on the left-hand side of the screen, use the following line of code:

```
self.navigationItem.setLeftBarButtonItem(button_item)
```

The status bar

The status bar is a 20-pixel bar that appears at the top of the window. It shows important system information, such as the signal strength, network, current time, and battery status.

By default, a status bar in iOS 6.0 comes in a translucent black style, but we can modify this look with the following available styles:

- `UIStatusBarStyleDefault`
- `UIStatusBarStyleBlackOpaque`
- `UIStatusBarStyleBlackTranslucent`

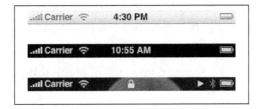

With RubyMotion, we can customize the status bar in the following two ways:

- **With Rakefile**: There is a setting in the `Rakefile` of your RubyMotion project; update it in the following way:

  ```
  app.status_bar_style = :black_translucent
  ```

- **With app code**: Update your delegate file with the following code snippet:

  ```
  application.setStatusBarStyle(UIStatusBarStyleBlackOpaque,
  animated:true)
  ```

 Note that these ways are distinct. The first one sets the status bar appearance while the application is being loaded, whereas the second one is used when the application has loaded.

The following code snippet shows how we can hide the status bar:

```
application.setStatusBarHidden(true,   withAnimation:UIStatusBarAnimat
ionSlide)
```

> As per Apple's guidelines, it is not advisable to create a custom status bar as users appreciate the consistency of the system-provided status bar.

Basic UI elements

In the previous section, we learned about bars, which play a pivotal role in creating the application view, primarily in the header and footer section of the screen. In this section, we will learn about other user interface elements essential for creating an interactive view. We will not discuss all the UI elements, however, as there are too many of them; we will examine only those that are used most frequently.

Label

A label displays a read-only text view and is used to display information. With the iOS SDK, we make use of the UILabel class to generate labels on screen. The UILabel class has many properties for customizing a label. In the following example, we will use a few of these properties to make our own customized label:

1. First, update the tab1_controller.rb file with following code inside the app folder:

```
def viewDidLoad
      view.backgroundColor = UIColor.
scrollViewTexturedBackgroundColor
      setupNavigationBar
      add_form_elements
    end
```

2. Next, add the add_form_elements method:

```
def add_form_elements
    label = UILabel.alloc.init
    label.frame = [[0, 40], [300, 30]]
    label.backgroundColor = UIColor.clearColor
    label.textColor = UIColor.greenColor
    label.font = UIFont.fontWithName("HelveticaNeue-
CondensedBold",size:18)
```

```
    label.text = "This is sample application"

    view.addSubview(label)
end
```

3. Let's fire up the terminal and test our app:

    $rake

4. We will see the following customized label appear on the screen:

Textfield

A `UITextField` object will create a textbox in the view. It is a very common input type in any form. This is how we create it:

1. Update the `add_form_elements` method in the `tab1_controller.rb` file:

    ```
    @textbox = UITextField.alloc.initWithFrame([[10,80],[200,35]])
    @textbox.borderStyle = UITextBorderStyleRoundedRect
    @textbox.placeholder = "Type.."
    @textbox.textAlignment = UITextAlignmentCenter
    view.addSubview(@textbox)
    ```

2. Let's fire up the terminal and test our app:

    $rake

3. We will see the following textbox appear on the screen:

> When a user taps the text field, the system automatically displays an associated keyboard. As the keyboard pops up from below, there is a chance that this will lead to an obscure view. It is the developer's duty to reposition the view accordingly.

Switch button

A UISwitch object will create a button to select on and off states. This is like a radio button that we commonly see when switching the Wi-Fi on and off. Follow the ensuing steps to create a switch button in your app:

1. Add the following code in tab1_controller.rb for the add_form_elements method inside the app folder:

```
@switch = UISwitch.alloc.initWithFrame([[10, 130], [200, 35]])
    @switch.addTarget(self,action:'switchIsChanged', forControlEve
nts:UIControlEventValueChanged)
    view.addSubview(@switch)
```

2. Once the button is switched from one state to another, it calls an action. Let's create the switchIsChanged action, which we already mentioned in the preceding step:

```
def switchIsChanged
if @switch.on?
  #Some code
else
 #some code
end
```

3. Let's fire up the terminal and test our app:

```
$rake
```

4. We will see the following switch button appear on the screen:

Slider

A UISlider object is a visual control used to select a single value from a continuous range of values. Sliders are always displayed as horizontal bars. Perform the following steps to create a slider in your app:

1. Add the following code in tab1_controller.rb for the add_form_elements method:

```
@customSlider = UISlider.alloc.initWithFrame([[10, 160],[200,
35]])
    #Setting the minimum value of slider
    @customSlider.minimumValue = 0
    #Setting the maximum value of slider
```

```
@customSlider.maximumValue = 1000
#Setting the default value of slider
@customSlider.value = @customSlider.maximumValue/2
#Setting the action value of slider to sliderValueChanged
@customSlider.addTarget(self, action:'sliderValueChanged', for
ControlEvents:UIControlEventValueChanged)
view.addSubview(@customSlider)
```

2. In the preceding code, when the slider's value is changed, the sliderValueChanged action will be called. Let's add this action in our tab1_controller.rb file:

```
def sliderValueChanged
  #some code
end
```

3. Let's fire up the terminal and test our app:

```
$rake
```

4. We will see the following slider appear on the screen:

Button

The UIButton class implements a button on the touchscreen. A button catches touch events and performs an action when tapped. Follow the ensuing steps to create a button in your app:

1. Add the following code in tab1_controller.rb for the add_form_elements method:

```
@normalButton = UIButton.buttonWithType(UIButtonTypeRoundedRect)
@normalButton.frame = [[10,200],[200,35]]
@normalButton.setTitle("Click Me",
forState:UIControlStateNormal)
@normalButton.setTitle("You have clicked me", forState:UIControl
StateHighlighted)
@normalButton.setTitle(self, action:'buttonIsPressed', forContro
lEvents:UIControlEventTouchDown)
view.addSubview(@normalButton)
```

2. Let's fire up the terminal and test our app:

```
$rake
```

3. We will see the following button appear on the screen:

Picker view

A picker view is used to select a value from multiple options. It uses a representation that is like a spinning wheel or slot machine to show one or more series of values similar to a select box in web applications.

The `UIPickerView` class implements a picker view. Let's understand this by adding one to our application:

1. Update the `tab2_controller.rb` file with the highlighted code. Go through the comments (the lines prefixed with #) for a better understanding of what's happening in that section:

```ruby
class Tab2Controller < UIViewController
  def init
    super
    self.tabBarItem = UITabBarItem.alloc.initWithTabBarSystemItem(
UITabBarSystemItemSearch, tag: 1)
    self
  end
  def viewDidLoad

    view.backgroundColor = UIColor.redColor
   # creating an array of country names
    @countryNames = ['United States', 'France', 'India', 'China',
'Russia']

    #calling add_label_and_button method to create label and
button
    add_label_and_button
    #calling create_picker method to create piker
    @picker = create_picker
    view.addSubview(@picker)

  end

  def create_picker
    picker = UIPickerView.alloc.initWithFrame(CGRectMake(10,100,
220, 250))
```

```ruby
    picker.hidden = true
    picker.showsSelectionIndicator = true
    picker.dataSource = self
    picker.delegate = self
    picker
  end

  def add_label_and_button
    @label = UILabel.alloc.init
    @label.frame = [[10, 40], [300, 30]]
    @label.backgroundColor = UIColor.clearColor
    @label.text = "Value"
    view.addSubview(@label)

    @button = UIButton.buttonWithType(UIButtonTypeRoundedRect)
    @button.frame = [[120, 40], [150, 30]]
    @button.setTitle("Show Picker",forState:UIControlStateNormal)
    @button
    @button.addTarget(self,
    action: 'show_picker',
    forControlEvents:UIControlEventTouchUpInside)
    view.addSubview(@button)
  end

  def show_picker
    if @picker.isHidden
      @picker.hidden = false
      @button.setTitle("Hide Picker",forState:UIControlStateNorm
al)
    else
      @picker.hidden = true
      @button.setTitle("Show Picker",forState:UIControlStateNorm
al)
    end
  end

#This method returns number of components in picker.
  def numberOfComponentsInPickerView(pickerView)
    1
  end

#This method returns number of rows in picker.
  def pickerView(pickerView,numberOfRowsInComponent:component)
    @countryNames.count
```

```
      end


   #This method returns value of rows in picker
     def pickerView(pickerView, titleForRow:row,forComponent:compone
   nt)
       @countryNames[row]
     end

   #This method will be called when some value is selected in picker
     def pickerView(pickerView, didSelectRow:row,
   inComponent:component)
       @label.text = @countryNames[row]
     end

end
```

2. Now, let's run the application and click on the second tab to check what we have done so far:

    $rake

3. We can see a **Show Picker** button, and once we click on it, we can see a picker view that allows us to select a country:

Let's understand the picker code that we have created using the `UIPickerView` class:

```
picker = UIPickerView.alloc.initWithFrame(CGRectMake(10,100, 220,
250))
picker.hidden = true
picker.showsSelectionIndicator = true
picker.dataSource = self
picker.delegate = self
picker
```

We must always provide `dataSource` and `delegate` in a picker because `datasource` supplies the data and `delegate` supplies the behavior of the picker. In the preceding code, we concealed the picker using `picker.hidden = true` as it will be shown only when the user clicks on the button.

To create a picker, we have to create a minimum of three delegate methods:

- `numberOfComponentsInPickerView`: This is called by the `PickerView` control to identify the number of components, such as the selection wheels, that are to be displayed to the user:

  ```
  def numberOfComponentsInPickerView(pickerView)
      1
  end
  ```

  In our code, we return `1` as we only have one component to show.

- `numberOfRowsInComponent`: This informs the `PickerView` control about the number of rows that are present in a specified component:

  ```
  def     pickerView(pickerView,numberOfRowsInComponent:component)
      @countryNames.count
      end
  ```

  So, `@countryNames.count` will return the total number of countries in the array.

- `titleForRow`: It will be called by the `PickerView` control to identify the string that is to be displayed for a specified row in a specific component:

  ```
  def pickerView(pickerView, titleForRow:row,forComponent:component)
      @countryNames[row]
    end
  ```

  The `pickerView:titleForRow:forComponent` method gets called *n* number of times; here *n* is the number returned by `pickerView:numberOfRowsInCom ponent`.

We can also perform an action when we select any value from the picker view. This can be done using the pickerView(pickerView, didSelectRow:row, inComponent:component) delegate method, as shown in the following code:

```
def pickerView(pickerView, didSelectRow:row, inComponent:component)
    @label.text = @countryNames[row]
End
```

Here, we are changing the label message with the country name that we have selected from the picker.

Hands-on – add a Restro Application

So far in this chapter, we have learned about the different UI elements; it's now time to apply this knowledge to enhance our Restro Application.

Firstly, we will add a tab bar and a navigation bar in our Restro Application, followed by creating a view for showing the restaurant detail page:

1. Update app_delegate.rb with the highlighted code:

```
class AppDelegate
  def application(application, didFinishLaunchingWithOptions:launc
hOptions)
    @window = UIWindow.alloc.initWithFrame(UIScreen.mainScreen.
bounds)
    @window.makeKeyAndVisible
    about_tab = UINavigationController.alloc.initWithRootViewCont
roller(AboutController.alloc.init)
    restro_tab = RestroController.alloc.initWithStyle(UITableViewS
tylePlain)
    restro_tab.tabBarItem = UITabBarItem.alloc.initWithTabBarSyste
mItem(UITabBarSystemItemSearch, tag: 1)
    @tabbar = UITabBarController.alloc.init
    @tabbar.viewControllers = [ restro_tab, about_tab]
    @tabbar.wantsFullScreenLayout = true
    @window.rootViewController = @tabbar
    true
  end
end
```

Here, we created a tab bar using `UITabBarController` and assigned two controllers, namely `RestroController` and `AboutController`, to it.

2. Next, let's create an `about_controller.rb` file in the `app` folder and add the following code:

```
class AboutController < UIViewController
def init
 if super
 self.tabBarItem.title = "About"
 self.tabBarItem.image = UIImage.imageNamed('FirstTab.png')
 end
super
end
def viewDidLoad
       view.backgroundColor = UIColor.whiteColor
       @label = UILabel.new
       @label.text = 'Restro Application'
       @label.lineBreakMode = UILineBreakModeWordWrap;
       @label.numberOfLines = 0
       @label.frame = [[50,50],[250,50]]
       view.addSubview(@label)

end
end
```

Here, we just created a simple view and added a label as a subview.

3. Now let's run the application to see our progress:

```
$rake
```

4. Here is the output we get:

> In the preceding screenshot, we can see a tab bar at the bottom of the screen with two tabs: **Search** and **About**.

In the last chapter, we implemented a search based on city. Let's make the search results on the search page clickable; this will redirect us to a new view that shows us the details of the restaurant that was selected:

1. Create a controller `detail_controller.rb` in the `app` folder:

```
class DetailController <  UIViewController
 attr_accessor :restaurant
  def viewDidLoad
    view.backgroundColor = UIColor.whiteColor
    show_restaurant_detail
  end
  def show_restaurant_detail
    label = UILabel.alloc.init
    label.frame = [[120, 20], [300, 30]]
    label.backgroundColor = UIColor.clearColor
    label.font = UIFont.fontWithName("HelveticaNeue-
CondensedBold",size:22)
```

```
        label.text = @restaurant.name
        view.addSubview(label)

        image = UIImage.alloc.initWithData(NSData.alloc.
initWithContentsOfURL(NSURL.URLWithString(@restaurant.thumb_url_
image)))
        view.addSubview(UIImageView.alloc.initWithImage(image))

        label = UILabel.alloc.init
        label.frame = [[20, 100], [300, 30]]
        label.backgroundColor = UIColor.clearColor
        label.font = UIFont.fontWithName("HelveticaNeue-
CondensedBold",size:15)
        label.text = @restaurant.desc
        view.addSubview(label)
    end
end
```

In these lines of code, we are showing all the details on the view that will get stored in the `@restaurant` instance variable from `RestroController`.

2. Add the following code in `restro_controller.rb` in the app folder:

```
def tableView(tableView, didSelectRowAtIndexPath:indexPath)
detail_controller = DetailController.alloc.init
    detail_controller.restaurant = @restaurants[indexPath.row]
    self.navigationController.pushViewController(detail_
controller,
      animated:true)
  end
```

This code will make each row of the table a link that will redirect to a detailed view.

3. Also, we need to replace the following line in `app_delegate.rb`:

```
RestroController.alloc.initWithStyle(UITableViewStylePlain)
```

4. The following code snippet will add a navigation bar with controls to enable easy navigation in between pages:

```
restro_tab = UINavigationController.alloc.initWithRootViewControll
er(RestroController.alloc.initWithStyle(UITableViewStylePlain))
```

5. Let's fire up the terminal, and check our progress:

$rake

6. This is the output we get:

7. We can see a navigation bar and a search bar, but we only need a search bar at the top. Let's make that change in `restro_application.rb` by replacing `view.tableHeaderView = searchBar` with what follows:

   ```
   self.navigationItem.titleView = searchBar
   ```

8. Generally in an iOS application, if a row is a link to another controller, an arrow is shown in the right-hand side corner. Let's add an arrow and make it look more like an iOS app. Update `restro_controller.rb`, and add the following line where we will create the `TableView` cell:

   ```
   cell.accessoryType = UITableViewCellAccessoryDisclosureIndicator
   ```

9. Let's run the application to check what we have done:

   ```
   $rake
   ```

10. We can see that the top navigation toolbar has disappeared, but arrows at the end of each row of the table view have appeared:

Summary

In this chapter, we have learned some of the fundamentals of the iOS user interface that are essential in creating outstanding user-friendly applications; we covered the following:

- We started by understanding standard UI elements, such as bars, and learned how to use them so that we do not lose the fundamental structure of an iOS app

- Next, we covered UI elements, such as textboxes, labels, sliders, pickers, and many more

- Lastly, we encompassed what we have learned so far in our application to get some real-time experience

In the next chapter, we will move our focus to using the powerful device capabilities of iOS devices and learn how to use them with RubyMotion. We will also learn how to make use of the camera, geolocation, contacts, gestures and many more features to create some amazing demo applications.

6
Device Capability – Power Unleashed

"Software will give you respect, but hardware will give you the Power."

- Akshat Paul

An iPhone is not only used for making calls, surfing the Internet, and playing music, but it is also the most advanced piece of hardware that can be used to take pictures, know your present location, comprehend gestures, and to do so many other things. So why not take advantage of these incredible device capabilities in your application. The beauty of these features is that just by tapping into the tools that the iPhone SDK provides, one can quickly import pictures, locations, and maps with minimal lines of code.

In this chapter we will focus on the following topics:

- Camera
- Location Manager (GPS)
- Gestures
- Core Data
- Address Book

Camera – smile please!

The camera is probably the most widely used feature of an iOS device. In this section, we will cover the most frequently used Camera events by creating an application that will allow us to take a picture using the Camera device and to select a picture from the Gallery.

An iPhone implements image selection through a picker that allows us to get images from different sources, such as Camera Roll or Photo Library. The `UIImagePickerController` class provides basic, customizable user interfaces (UIs) for taking pictures and videos, also providing the user with some simple editing capabilities for newly captured media.

The role and appearance of a `UIImagePickerController` class depends on the value of `sourceType` assigned to it. There are three ways to choose the source of an image, as follows:

- Choose from Camera:

  ```
  imagePicker.sourceType = UIImagePickerControllerSourceTypeCamera;
  ```

- Choose from any folder in Gallery:

  ```
  imagePicker.sourceType =
  UIImagePickerControllerSourceTypePhotoLibrary;
  ```

- Choose from Photo Album (Camera Roll):

  ```
  imagePicker.sourceType =
  UIImagePickerControllerSourceTypeSavedPhotosAlbum;
  ```

Camera example

Let's create an application that will allow us to capture a photo from the camera and select an image from Photo Gallery. Perform the following steps:

1. Create an application with the `motion` command:

   ```
   motion create CameraExample
   ```

2. Update `app_delegate.rb` and set the root controller to `CameraController`:

   ```
   class AppDelegate
     def application(application, didFinishLaunchingWithOptions:launc
   hOptions)
       @window = UIWindow.alloc.initWithFrame(UIScreen.mainScreen.
   bounds)
       @window.rootViewController = CameraController.alloc.init
       @window.makeKeyAndVisible
       true
     end
   end
   ```

3. Create a file named `camera_controller.rb` inside the app folder:

```ruby
class CameraController < UIViewController

  def viewDidLoad
    view.backgroundColor = UIColor.underPageBackgroundColor
    load_view
  end

  def load_view
    @camera_button = UIButton.buttonWithType(UIButtonTypeRoundedRe
ct)
    @camera_button.frame   = [[50, 20], [200, 50]]
    @camera_button.setTitle("Click from camera",
forState:UIControlStateNormal)
    @camera_button.addTarget(self, action: :start_camera, forContr
olEvents:UIControlEventTouchUpInside)
    view.addSubview(@camera_button)

    @gallery_button = UIButton.buttonWithType(UIButtonTypeRoundedR
ect)
    @gallery_button.frame   = [[50, 100], [200, 50]]
    @gallery_button.setTitle("Chose from Gallery",
forState:UIControlStateNormal)
    @gallery_button.addTarget(self, action: :open_gallery, forCont
rolEvents:UIControlEventTouchUpInside)
    view.addSubview(@gallery_button)

    @image_picker = UIImagePickerController.alloc.init
    @image_picker.delegate = self
  end

  def imagePickerController(picker, didFinishPickingImage:image,
editingInfo:info)
    self.dismissModalViewControllerAnimated(true)
    @image_view.removeFromSuperview if @image_view
    @image_view = UIImageView.alloc.initWithImage(image)
    @image_view.frame = [[50, 200], [200, 180]]
    view.addSubview(@image_view)
  end

  def start_camera
    if camera_present?
      @image_picker.sourceType =
UIImagePickerControllerSourceTypeCamera
      presentModalViewController(@image_picker, animated:true)
    else
      show_alert
    end
  end
```

```
def open_gallery
  @image_picker.sourceType =
UIImagePickerControllerSourceTypePhotoLibrary
  presentModalViewController(@image_picker, animated:true)
end
def show_alert
  alert = UIAlertView.new
  alert.message = 'No Camera in device'
  alert.show
end
def camera_present?
  UIImagePickerController.isSourceTypeAvailable(UIImagePickerCon
trollerSourceTypeCamera)
end
end
```

Let's see what we have done so far by testing our application on the simulator using the following command:

$rake

We can see the results as shown in the following screenshot:

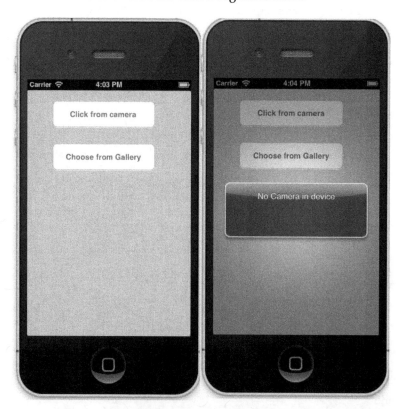

As we are using an iPhone simulator, we cannot access the camera hardware. However, if we test our application with an iPhone device, we will be able to use the camera hardware and capture images from it. Now let's choose an image from Gallery by clicking on the **Choose from Gallery** button:

Understanding the Camera code

First, we need to initiate two buttons for the photo-taking process and choose a picture from Gallery. We will also create an image picker:

```
def load_view
  @camera_button = UIButton.buttonWithType(UIButtonTypeRoundedRect)
  @camera_button.frame  = [[50, 20], [200, 50]]
  @camera_button.setTitle("Click from camera",
forState:UIControlStateNormal)
  @camera_button.addTarget(self, action: :start_camera, forControlEv
ents:UIControlEventTouchUpInside)
  view.addSubview(@camera_button)
```

```
    @gallery_button = UIButton.buttonWithType(UIButtonTypeRoundedRect)
    @gallery_button.frame = [[50, 100], [200, 50]]
    @gallery_button.setTitle("Choose from Gallery",
forState:UIControlStateNormal)
    @gallery_button.addTarget(self, action: :open_gallery, forControlE
vents:UIControlEventTouchUpInside)
    view.addSubview(@gallery_button)

    @image_picker = UIImagePickerController.alloc.init
    @image_picker.delegate = self
  end
```

So when we click on the **Click from camera** and **Choose from Gallery** buttons, the start_camera and open_gallery actions will be called, respectively:

```
  def start_camera
    if camera_present?
      @image_picker.sourceType =
UIImagePickerControllerSourceTypeCamera
      presentModalViewController(@image_picker, animated:true)
    else
      show_alert
    end
  end

  def open_gallery
    @image_picker.sourceType =
UIImagePickerControllerSourceTypePhotoLibrary
    presentModalViewController(@image_picker, animated:true)
  end
  def show_alert
    alert = UIAlertView.new
    alert.message = 'No Camera in device'
    alert.show
  end
```

So we have used UIImagePickerControllerSourceTypeCamera and UIImagePickerControllerSourceTypePhotoLibrary as source types; they will open the Camera and Photo Library tools, respectively.

As an iOS application can also be installed on devices such as an iPod, which does not have a camera, to check the device for a camera, the UIImagePickerController.isSourceTypeAvailable(UIImageP ickerControllerSourceTypeCamera) method is used.

The following two camera picker delegates are available:

- `imagePickerController:didFinishPickingImage:` This is called when the image is selected

- `imagePickerControllerDidCancel`: This is called when the **Cancel** button is clicked

The following delegate will be called when an image is selected:

```
def imagePickerController(picker, didFinishPickingImage:image,
editingInfo:info)
    self.dismissModalViewControllerAnimated(true)
    @image_view.removeFromSuperview if @image_view
    @image_view = UIImageView.alloc.initWithImage(image)
    @image_view.frame = [[50, 200], [200, 180]]
    view.addSubview(@image_view)
end
```

The `self.dismissModalViewControllerAnimated(true)` method is called explicitly to remove the pop-up, and then the image is displayed using `UIImageView`.

Location Manager – directions for apps

You must have observed that in many iOS applications, your current location is spotted automatically. With RubyMotion, we can easily use the location capabilities of your device with our application. There are two parts to this: the first is to find the device location and the second is to display it in our application.

iOS SDK contains various layers; one of them is the **Core Services** layer and a part of this layer is the **Core Location** framework. This framework uses the available hardware to determine a user's current position and where they are heading. Core Location provides us with coordinates, text strings, and number values instead of visual location information such as maps. Later in the chapter, we will also use Map Kit that will help us embed maps directly in our views using our knowledge of the Core Location framework.

Location Manager example

Let's create an application to demonstrate how we can use Location Manager with the RubyMotion application. Perform the following steps:

1. Create an application with the `motion` command:

   ```
   $motion create LocationManager
   ```

2. Update the `app_delegate.rb` file:

```
class AppDelegate
  def application(application, didFinishLaunchingWithOptions:launc
hOptions)
     @window = UIWindow.alloc.initWithFrame(UIScreen.mainScreen.
bounds)
     @window.rootViewController = LocationController.alloc.init
     @window.makeKeyAndVisible
    true
  end
end
```

3. Update the `rake` file and add the following line of code:

```
app.frameworks = ['CoreLocation', 'MapKit']
```

4. To use the Location service, we have to include the following two frameworks:

   ° CoreLocation: The `CoreLocation` framework lets you determine the current location. This framework uses the available hardware of the device to determine the device's current position and where it is heading.

   ° MapKit: The `MapKit` framework provides an interface for embedding maps directly into your app's views.

5. Create the `location_controller.rb` controller in the `app` folder and add the following code:

```
class LocationController < UIViewController
  def viewDidLoad
    view.backgroundColor = UIColor.underPageBackgroundColor
    create_location_label
    check_location

  end

  def check_location
    if (CLLocationManager.locationServicesEnabled)
    @location_manager = CLLocationManager.alloc.init
    @location_manager.desiredAccuracy =
KCLLocationAccuracyKilometer
    @location_manager.delegate = self
    @location_manager.purpose = " Our applications functionality
```

```
is based on your current location "
    @location_manager.startUpdatingLocation
  else
    show_error_message('Please enable the Location Services for
this app in Settings.')
  end
end
def create_location_label
@latitudeLabel = UILabel.alloc.initWithFrame( [[25, 30], [250,
40]] )
@latitudeLabel.backgroundColor = UIColor.clearColor

@longitudeLabel = UILabel.alloc.initWithFrame( [[25, 80], [250,
40]] )
@longitudeLabel.backgroundColor = UIColor.clearColor

  @latitudeLabel.text = "Latitude:"
  @longitudeLabel.text = "Longitude:"
  view.addSubview(@latitudeLabel)
  view.addSubview(@longitudeLabel)
end
def locationManager(manager, didUpdateToLocation:newLocation,
fromLocation:oldLocation)
  @latitudeLabel.text =  @latitudeLabel.text + newLocation.
coordinate.latitude.to_s
  @longitudeLabel.text =  @longitudeLabel.text + newLocation.
coordinate.longitude.to_s
  end

  def locationManager(manager, didFailWithError:error)

    show_error_message('Please enable the Location Services for
this app in Settings.')
  end
  def show_error_message msg
    alert = UIAlertView.new
    alert.message =  msg
    alert.show
  end

end
```

In the preceding code, we configured the CLLocationManager object using the following steps:

1. Always check to see whether the desired services are available before starting any service and abandon the operation if they are not. You can do so by triggering CLLocationManager.locationServicesEnable. If this returns true, the service has been enabled for your application.

    The user has the option of denying applications the ability to access its Location service data. During the initial use by an application, the Core Location framework prompts the user to confirm that using the Location service is acceptable. If the user denies the request, the CLLocationManager object reports an appropriate error to the delegate in future requests.

2. Then we created an instance of the CLLocationManager class:

    ```
    @location_manager = CLLocationManager.alloc.init
    ```

3. Next, we configured additional properties relevant to the Location service:

    ```
    @location_manager.desiredAccuracy =
    KCLLocationAccuracyKilometer
    ```

    desiredAccuracy supports a wide range of methods that provide different levels of accuracy. You can also use KCLLocationAccuracyBest; it will give you more accurate results but it will also drain the battery. KCLLocationAccuracyKilometer doesn't give an accurate location but is more effective in terms of performance.

    ```
    @location_manager.delegate = self
    ```

    ```
    @location_manager.purpose = "Our application provides
    functionality based on your current location"
    ```

    This message will appear when the application asks for permissions.

4. Then we created a delegate to handle the latitude and longitude for our application:

    ```
    def locationManager(manager, didUpdateToLocation:newLocation,
    fromLocation:oldLocation)
        @latitudeLabel.text =  @latitudeLabel.text + newLocation.
    coordinate.latitude.to_s
        @longitudeLabel.text =  @longitudeLabel.text + newLocation.
    coordinate.longitude.to_s
      end
    ```

5. Lastly, we called the appropriate start method to begin the delivery of events:

```
@location_manager.startUpdatingLocation
```

Let's fire up the terminal and test our app using the following command:

```
$rake
```

The output is as follows:

If your location is not set in your simulator, you will get a pop-up showing an error, as shown in the preceding screenshot.

As we are using the iOS simulator, we do not have physical GPS access for the iPhone device. However, iOS simulator does give us the option to mimic this by selecting or adding values via the emulator. From the toolbar, navigate to **Debug | Location** and either choose or add custom longitude and latitude values.

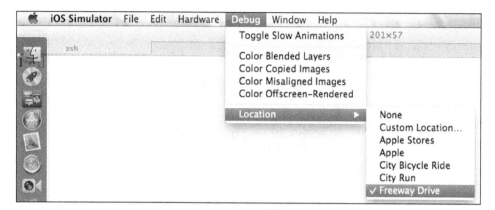

You can see a pop-up on the screen with a custom message, which we had described in our code:

Once we click on **OK**, we will see the longitude and latitude of our current location as shown in the following screenshot:

Now let's plot the current location on a map and display this on our screen.

1. Add the following code to the `location_controller.rb` file in the app folder:

```
def show_map
    map= MKMapView.alloc.initWithFrame( [[20,190], [275, 150]] )
    map.mapType = MKMapTypeStandard
    self.view.addSubview(map)
end
```

We have chosen `MKMapTypeStandard`, but `MKMapView` provides the following three types of maps:

- ○ `MKMapTypeStandard`: This shows a street and some road names
- ○ `MKMapTypeSatellite`: This shows satellite imagery
- ○ `MKMapTypeHybrid`: This shows a satellite image of the area with roads and their names along with other information superimposed

2. Then, add the following code in the `viewDidLoad` method in the `location_controller.rb` file:

```
def viewDidLoad
  view.backgroundColor = UIColor.underPageBackgroundColor
  location_label
  check_location
  show_map
end
```

3. Now run the application in the simulator using the following command:

```
$rake
```

The output is as follows:

The preceding code will only show a map on the screen and not pinpoint the location. We are now going to add a pin—annotations in MapKit terms—to our map.

4. Update the `show_map` method in the `location_controller.rb` file:

```
def show_map
  map= MKMapView.alloc.initWithFrame( [[20,190], [275, 150]] )
  map.mapType = MKMapTypeStandard
  location = CLLocationCoordinate2D.new(@latitude, @longitude)
  map.setRegion( MKCoordinateRegionMake(location,
MKCoordinateSpanMake(1, 1)),animated:true )
  pointer = MyAnnotation.alloc.initWithCoordinate(location,
title:"Title", andSubTitle:"Sub Title")
  map.addAnnotation(pointer)
  self.view.addSubview(map)
end
```

`CLLocationCoordinate2D` is a structure that contains the geographical coordinate of a location.

5. To add the pin (Annotation), you must create a class that explicitly implements the `MKAnnotation` protocol. We should define the following attributes in this class:

   ° coordinate

   ° title

   ° subtitle

6. Let's create a file named `my_annotation.rb` inside the `app` folder. Create a class named `MyAnnotation` that has these attributes:

```
class MyAnnotation
  def initWithCoordinate(coordinate, title:title,
andSubTitle:subtitle)
    @coordinate = coordinate
    @title = title
    @subtitle = subtitle
    self
  end

  def coordinate
    @coordinate
  end
  def title
    @title
  end
```

```
      def subtitle
        @subtitle
      end
end
```

7. Update the `location_controller.rb` file with the following code:

```
    def locationManager(manager, didUpdateToLocation:newLocation,
fromLocation:oldLocation)
        @latitude = newLocation.coordinate.latitude
        @longitude = newLocation.coordinate.longitude
        @latitudeLabel.text =  @latitudeLabel.text + newLocation.
coordinate.latitude.to_s
        @longitudeLabel.text =  @longitudeLabel.text + newLocation.
coordinate.longitude.to_s
        @location_manager.stopUpdatingLocation
        show_map
    end
```

8. Let's fire up the terminal and run our application using the
    following command:

    `$rake`

    The output is as follows:

In the preceding screenshot, we can see a map with the current location and its description.

 You can change the location in the simulator by navigating to **Debug | Change Location**.

Gestures – non-verbal communication

Gestures are a big part of iOS applications. For example, when we pinch on a picture, it gets zoomed, or when we rotate our device, the orientation of the picture changes. Detecting gestures in your application is very easy with the built-in UIGestureRecognizer classes.

There are a few subclasses of UIGestureRecognizer, each designed to detect a specific type of gesture. You can handle the most commonly used gestures with the following subclasses:

- UITapGestureRecognizer: This class detects the tapping gesture made on the device screen by the user.

- UIPinchGestureRecognizer: This class detects the pinching gesture made on screen by the user. This motion is usually used to zoom in or out of a view or to change the size of a visual component.

- UIPanGestureRecognizer: This class detects the dragging or panning gesture that the user makes.

- UISwipeGestureRecognizer: This class detects when the user makes a swiping gesture across the screen. Instances of this class may be configured to detect motion only in a specific direction.

- UIRotationGestureRecognizer: This class identifies the rotation gesture that the user makes. (To make a rotation gesture, move two fingers located opposite each other in contact with the screen and move them in a circular motion.)

- UILongPressGestureRecognizer: This class is used to identify when the user touches the screen with one or more fingers for a specified period of time.

Gesture example

The following is an example of how the gesture feature can be used:

1. Create an application that will help us understand the various gestures we have discussed in the last section:

   ```
   $motion create gesture
   ```

2. Update the `app_delegate.rb` file in the `app` folder:

   ```
   class AppDelegate
     def application(application, didFinishLaunchingWithOptions:launchOptions)

           @window = UIWindow.alloc.initWithFrame(UIScreen.mainScreen.bounds)
           @window.rootViewController = UINavigationController.alloc.initWithRootViewController(GestureController.new)
           @window.makeKeyAndVisible
       true
     end
   end
   ```

3. Now, create a file named `gesture_controller.rb` in the `app` folder and add the following code:

   ```
   class GestureController <  UIViewController
     def viewDidLoad
       view.backgroundColor = UIColor.whiteColor

       longPressRecognizer = UILongPressGestureRecognizer.alloc.initWithTarget(self, action:'longPressGestureRecognizer:')
       tap_gesture_recognizer = UITapGestureRecognizer.alloc.initWithTarget(self,action:'tabGestureRecognizer:')
       rotate_gesture_recognizer = UIRotationGestureRecognizer.alloc.initWithTarget(self, action:'rotationGestureRecognizer:')
       swipe_gesture_recognizer = UISwipeGestureRecognizer.alloc.initWithTarget(self, action:'swipeGestureRecognizer:')
       pan_gesture_recognizer = UIPanGestureRecognizer.alloc.initWithTarget(self, action:'panGestureRecognizer:')
       pinch_gesture_recognizer = UIPinchGestureRecognizer.alloc.initWithTarget(self, action:'pinchGestureRecognizer:')

       self.view.addGestureRecognizer(longPressRecognizer)
       self.view.addGestureRecognizer(tap_gesture_recognizer)
       self.view.addGestureRecognizer(rotate_gesture_recognizer)
       self.view.addGestureRecognizer(swipe_gesture_recognizer)
   ```

```ruby
    self.view.addGestureRecognizer(pan_gesture_recognizer)
    self.view.addGestureRecognizer(pinch_gesture_recognizer)
    load_labels
  end
    def longPressGestureRecognizer(longPressRecognizer)
    show_alert("You've pressed the screen long enough!") if
UIGestureRecognizerStateEnded == longPressRecognizer.state
  end
  def tabGestureRecognizer(tap_gesture_recognizer)
    show_alert("You've tapped the screen!")
  end
  def rotationGestureRecognizer(rotate_gesture_recognizer)
    show_alert("You've rotated the screen!") if
UIGestureRecognizerStateEnded == rotate_gesture_recognizer.state
  end
  def swipeGestureRecognizer(swipe_gesture_recognizer)
    show_alert("You've just swiped!") if
UIGestureRecognizerStateEnded == swipe_gesture_recognizer.state
  end
  def panGestureRecognizer(pan_gesture_recognizer)
    show_alert("You've Panned!") if UIGestureRecognizerStateEnded
== pan_gesture_recognizer.state
  end
  def pinchGestureRecognizer(pinch_gesture_recognizer)
    show_alert("You've Pinched!") if UIGestureRecognizerStateEnded
== pinch_gesture_recognizer.state
  end

  def load_labels
    label = UILabel.new
    label.frame = [[10,50],[300,100]]
    label.lineBreakMode = UILineBreakModeWordWrap;
    label.numberOfLines = 0
    label.text = " Try a different gesture such as tap, rotate,
swipe, pan and pinch "
    view.addSubview(label)
  end
  def show_alert(message)
    alert_box = UIAlertView.alloc.initWithTitle("Gesture Action",
    message:message,
    delegate: nil,
    cancelButtonTitle: "ok",
    otherButtonTitles:nil)

    alert_box.show
  end
end
```

4. Run the application using the following command:

`$rake`

The output is as follows:

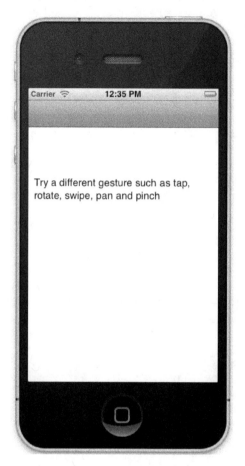

 You must be wondering how we can use multi-touch on a simulator. To use this feature on a simulator, hold the *Option* key; doing this will display two circles on the simulator screen. You can move them in the desired direction.

Now let's understand the code. First, we created a different recognizer for each class:

```
    longPressRecognizer = UILongPressGestureRecognizer.alloc.
initWithTarget(self, action:'longPressGestureRecognizer:')
    tap_gesture_recognizer = UITapGestureRecognizer.alloc.initWithTarg
et(self,action:'tabGestureRecognizer:')
    rotate_gesture_recognizer = UIRotationGestureRecognizer.alloc.
initWithTarget(self, action:'rotationGestureRecognizer:')
    swipe_gesture_recognizer = UISwipeGestureRecognizer.alloc.
initWithTarget(self, action:'swipeGestureRecognizer:')
    pan_gesture_recognizer = UIPanGestureRecognizer.alloc.
initWithTarget(self, action:'panGestureRecognizer:')
    pinch_gesture_recognizer = UIPinchGestureRecognizer.alloc.
initWithTarget(self, action:'pinchGestureRecognizer:')
```

For each recognizer, we'll call an action. This means that whenever the user creates a pattern or makes a gesture, such as a rotation, its corresponding action is called. For example, when a user tries to pinch the view, `pinchGestureRecognizer` gets called.

Remember that after we have created the recognizers, we need to add them to the view so that users can interact with them. We did this by adding them to the `addGestureRecognizer()` method by passing the recognizer object to the view:

```
self.view.addGestureRecognizer(longPressRecognizer)
self.view.addGestureRecognizer(tap_gesture_recognizer)
self.view.addGestureRecognizer(rotate_gesture_recognizer)
self.view.addGestureRecognizer(swipe_gesture_recognizer)
self.view.addGestureRecognizer(pan_gesture_recognizer)
self.view.addGestureRecognizer(pinch_gesture_recognizer)
```

Next, we created actions for each gesture. We are just showing a pop-up when the user shows any of the common gestures. For example, when we pinch, the following code is called:

```
def pinchGestureRecognizer(pinch_gesture_recognizer)
    show_alert("You have Pinch") if UIGestureRecognizerStateEnded ==
pinch_gesture_recognizer.state
  end
```

This action is called in several states, such as when pinching starts and when pinching stops. For discrete gestures, such as a tapping gesture, the gesture recognizer invokes the method once per recognition; for continuous gestures, the gesture recognizer invokes the method at repeated intervals until the gesture ends (that is, until the last finger is lifted from the gesture recognizer's view). So, there can be many states that you can find by `UIGestureRecognizerState`. Its value can be one of the following:

- `UIGestureRecognizerStatePossible`
- `UIGestureRecognizerStateBegan`
- `UIGestureRecognizerStateChanged`
- `UIGestureRecognizerStateEnded`
- `UIGestureRecognizerStateCancelled`
- `UIGestureRecognizerStateFailed`
- `UIGestureRecognizerStateRecognized =` `UIGestureRecognizerStateEnded`

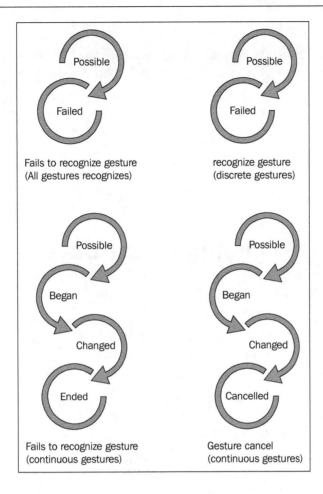

As shown in the preceding figure, when a gesture is recognized, every subsequent state transition causes an action message to be sent to the target. When a gesture recognizer reaches the **Recognized** or **Ended** state, it is asked to reset its internal state in preparation for a new attempt at recognizing the gesture.

Responses to the gestures should be in line with what the users expect. For example, a pinching gesture should scale a view, zooming it in and out; it should not be interpreted as, say, a selection request, for which a tap is more appropriate.

Do it yourself

You can implement your own custom gesture recognizer. To implement this, first create a subclass of UIGestureRecognizer. Then you can override the following methods:

- reset
- touchesBegan
- touchesMoved
- touchesEnded
- touchesCancelled

Core Data – manage your data

Sometimes applications are required to save and manipulate user data. iOS SDK provides a framework for this purpose known as Core Data.

The **Core Data** framework provides comprehensive and automated solutions related to an object's life cycle and its searching and persistence features. It can retrieve and manipulate data purely on an object level without having to worry about the details of storage and retrieval.

With Core Data, data can be handled using higher-level objects indicating entities and their relationships. Core Data interfaces directly with SQLite, separating the developer from the underlying SQL.

So does it mean Core Data is a database? No; Core Data is not a database and the best example of this is that Core Data can be used totally in memory without any form of persistence. Then is Core Data similar to an ORM such as Active Record or Hibernate? No; Core Data is an object graph manager with life cycle, searching, and persistence features. With Core Data, an app can define a database schema, create a database file, and create and manage record data.

Core Data example

We will create a simple employee application that will allow us to add the name and age of an employee. This example is only used to demonstrate how Core Data works:

1. Let's create an application using the motion command:

   ```
   $motion create CoreDataExample
   ```

2. Add the CoreData framework in the rake.rb file:

   ```
   app.frameworks += ['CoreData']
   ```

3. This will be an MVC application, so let's create a model named `employee.rb` in the app folder:

```
class Employee < NSManagedObject
  #Attribute Name, Data Type, Default Value, Is Optional, Is
Transient, Is Indexed
  @attributes ||= [
    ['name', NSStringAttributeType, '', false, false, false],
    ['age', NSInteger32AttributeType, 0, false, false, false]
  ]
end
```

You must have noticed that we have inherited the `Employee` class from `NSManagedObject`. We have created an array of arrays for attributes in the `employee` table with the attributes `name` and `age`. You must be wondering what other parameters there are in this array. To understand this, we will have to write a few helpers in our application.

4. Let's create a folder named `helper` and add a file named `NSEntityDescription.rb` with the following code in it:

```
class NSEntityDescription
  def self.newEntityDescriptionWithName(name,
attributes:attributes)
    entity = self.alloc.init
    entity.name = name
    entity.managedObjectClassName = name

    attributes = attributes.each.map do |name, type, default,
optional, transient, indexed|
      property = NSAttributeDescription.alloc.init
      property.name = name
      property.attributeType = type
      property.defaultValue = default if default != nil
      property.optional = optional
      property.transient = transient
      property.indexed = indexed
      property
    end
    entity.properties = attributes
    entity
  end
end
```

The attributes that we have created in the employee model are defined through this class. For each attribute, the NSAttributeDescription class will be used to define them. The NSAttributeDescription class is used to describe attributes of an entity described by an instance of NSEntityDescription. It is inherited from NSPropertyDescription, which provides most of the basic behavior. Instances of NSAttributeDescription are used to describe attributes, as distinct from relationships. We can define many properties for an object of NSAttributeDescription; for example, we can put a validation on it, we can index the attribute, and much more.

5. Next, create a file named NSManagedObject.rb in the app folder and add the following code:

```
def self.entity
  @entity ||= NSEntityDescription.newEntityDescriptionWithName(n
ame, attributes:@attributes)
  end

def self.objects
  # Use if you do not want any section in your table view
  @objects ||= NSFetchRequest.fetchObjectsForEntity
ForName(name, withSortKey:@sortKey, ascending:false,
inManagedObjectContext:Store.shared.context)
  end

end

class NSManagedObject
  def self.entity
    @entity ||= NSEntityDescription.newEntityDescriptionWithName(n
ame, attributes:@attributes)
  end
  def self.objects
    # Use if you do not want any section in your table view
    @objects ||= NSFetchRequest.fetchObjectsForEntity
ForName(name, withSortKey:@sortKey, ascending:false,
inManagedObjectContext:Store.shared.context)
  end
end
```

An NSEntityDescription object describes an entity in Core Data. An entity to a manage object is what a class is to an ID or, to use a database analogy, what tables are to rows. An NSEntityDescription object may have NSAttributeDescription and NSRelationshipDescription objects that represent the properties of the entity in the schema. An entity may also have fetched properties, represented by instances of NSFetchedPropertyDescription, and the model may have fetched request templates, represented by instances of NSFetchRequest.

6. Now, add the following code to the `app_delegate.rb` file:

```ruby
class AppDelegate
  def application(application, didFinishLaunchingWithOptions:launc
hOptions)
    setting_core_data
    true
  end

  def setting_core_data

    # First we need to create the NSManagedObjectModel with all
the entities and their relationships.
    managed_object_model = NSManagedObjectModel.alloc.init
    managed_object_model.entities = [Employee.entity]


    # The next object needed is the NSPersistentStoreCoordinator
which will allow Core Data to persist the information.
    persistent_store_coordinator = NSPersistentStoreCoordinator.
alloc.initWithManagedObjectModel(managed_object_model)

    # Now lets get a URL for where we want Core Data to create the
persist file, in this case a SQLite Database File
    persistent_store_file_url = NSURL.fileURLWithPath(File.
join(NSHomeDirectory(),

'Documents',

'EmployeeStore.sqlite'))


    error_pointer = Pointer.new(:object)

    # Add a new Persistent Store to our Persistent Store
Coordinator which means that we are telling the Persistent Store
Coordinator where to perform the save of our objects.
    # In this case we are stating that our objects must be stored
in a SQLite database in the path we already created previously
    unless persistent_store_coordinator.addPersistentStoreWithType(
NSSQLiteStoreType,
configuration: nil,
URL: persistent_store_file_url,
options: nil,
error: error_pointer)
```

```
      # In case we can't initialize the Persistance Store File
   raise "Cannot initialize Core Data Persistance Store Coordinator:
#{error_pointer[0].description}"
      end
      # Finally our most important object, the Managed Object
Context, is responsible for creating, destroying, and fetching the
objects

      @managed_object_context = NSManagedObjectContext.alloc.init
      @managed_object_context.persistentStoreCoordinator =
persistent_store_coordinator
   end
end
```

Till now we have done some basic settings that we are required to do before actually using database operations. In this case, we are stating that our objects must be stored in a SQLite database at a location we define in our code with the filename `EmployeeStore.sqlite`.

In the preceding code, we have created an object of `NSManagedObjectModel` with all the entities. You can think of this object as a reference of the objects to be used by Core Data. The next object needed is the `NSPersistentStoreCoordinator` object that will allow Core Data to persist the information. It is also responsible for choosing a location to save our objects.

In the last part of our code, we have used the most important class, which is the `NSManagedObjectContext` class. This class is responsible for creating, destroying, and fetching the objects. An instance of `NSManagedObjectContext` represents a single "object space" or scratch pad in an application. Its primary responsibility is to manage a collection of managed objects. These objects form a group of related model objects that represent an internally consistent view of one or more persistent stores. A single managed object instance exists in one and only one context, but multiple copies of an object can exist in different contexts.

7. Let's fire up the terminal and run our application using the following command:

   $rake

8. You will see a blank screen as we have not yet created the controller and view. We will create them in the next section, but before that, let's first update the `app_delegate` file to accommodate the controller and view with the following code:

```
def application(application, didFinishLaunchingWithOptions:launc
hOptions)
    setting_core_data
    employee_view_controller = EmployeeViewController.alloc.init

    # We need to pass the Managed Object Context to the next
controller so we can use it later for creating, fetching or
deleting objects
    employee_view_controller.managed_object_context = @managed_
object_context
```

```
        @window = UIWindow.alloc.initWithFrame(UIScreen.mainScreen.
bounds)
        @window.rootViewController = UINavigationController.alloc.
initWithRootViewController(employee_view_controller)
        @window.makeKeyAndVisible

        true
    end
```

Creating an employee

In the last part of the previous code snippet, we initialized
EmployeeViewController. Next, we will pass the managed object context to the
next controller that will later be used for either creating, fetching, or deleting objects.
And in the end, we will create a window and assign EmployeeViewController as its
root controller:

1. Create a file named employee_view_controller.rb in the app folder with
   the following code in it:

```
class EmployeeViewController < UIViewController
 attr_accessor :managed_object_context
 def loadView
   # Set up the title for the View Controller
   self.title = 'Employee'

   # Create a new Table View for showing the Text Fields
   table_view = UITableView.alloc.initWithFrame(UIScreen.
mainScreen.bounds,

style:UITableViewStyleGrouped)
   table_view.dataSource = self
   self.view = table_view

   # Create a new Bar Button Item with the Add System Default
   add_new_employee_item= UIBarButtonItem.alloc.initWithBarButtonS
ystemItem(UIBarButtonSystemItemAdd,

target: self,

action: 'add_new_employee')
   # Add the Bar Button Item to the Navigation Bar
   self.navigationItem.rightBarButtonItem = add_new_employee_item
 end
```

```
def viewWillAppear(animated)
  super
  reload_data
end
```

2. Next, let's fetch specific objects using the NSFetchRequest object. We also need to tell Core Data which entity we want to retrieve. This can be done using NSEntityDescription:

```
def reload_data
fetch_request = NSFetchRequest.alloc.init

entity = NSEntityDescription.entityForName(Employee.name,

inManagedObjectContext:@managed_object_context)
  fetch_request.setEntity(entity)

  # Sort the Employee by employee name
  fetch_sort = NSSortDescriptor.alloc.initWithKey('name',
                                                ascending:
true)
  fetch_request.setSortDescriptors([fetch_sort])

  # Update the fetch employee array and reload the table view
  update_fetched_employee_with_fetch_request(fetch_request)
end


def update_fetched_employee_with_fetch_request(fetch_request)

  # Create a new pointer for managing the errors
  error_pointer = Pointer.new(:object)

  # Using the NSManagedObjectContext execute the fetch request
  @fetched_employee = @managed_object_context.
executeFetchRequest(fetch_request,

error: error_pointer)

  # If the returning array of the fetch request is nil
  # means that a problem has occurred
  unless @fetched_employee
    raise "Error fetching employee: #{error_pointer[0].
description}"
  end
```

```
    # refresh table view to reload its data
    self.view.reloadData
  end


  # UITableView Data Source
  def tableView(tableView, numberOfRowsInSection: section)
    @fetched_employee.count
  end


  def tableView(tableView, cellForRowAtIndexPath: indexPath)
    cell_identifier = 'EmployeeCell'
    cell = tableView.dequeueReusableCellWithIdentifier(cell_
identifier)
    # If we are not cells to use we need to create one
    if cell == nil
      # Lets create a new UITableViewCell with the identifier
      cell = UITableViewCell.alloc.initWithStyle(UITableViewCellSty
leValue1, reuseIdentifier:cell_identifier)
      cell.selectionStyle = UITableViewCellSelectionStyleNone
    end

    employee = @fetched_employee[indexPath.row]
    cell.textLabel.text = employee.name
    cell.detailTextLabel.text = employee.age.to_s
    cell
  end


  def add_new_employee
    add_employee_view_controller = AddEmployeeViewController.alloc.
init

    # We need to pass the Managed Object Context to the next
controller so we can use it later for creating, fetching or
deleting objects
    add_employee_view_controller.managed_object_context = @managed_
object_context
    self.navigationController.pushViewController(add_employee_view_
controller,
                                                     animated:true)
  end

end
```

That's a lot of code; let's try to understand it. First, we created a `tableView` to create a table as it's the best way to represent this type of data. Then, we created a **+** button at the top of the navigation bar with the `add_new_employee` action associated with it. When this button is pressed, it calls the `add_new_employee` action that, in turn, calls a new view, shows a form, and adds a new employee.

Then, we created a `reload_data` method that will be called to refresh the view with employee data. It will fetch the employee data using the `NSFetchRequest` object. Then, we declared `NSEntityDescription` for the `Employee` object so we can tell Core Data which entity we want to retrieve. We also sorted the result by name using `NSSortDescriptor`.

In the last part of our example, we created an `update_fetched_employee_with_fetch_request` method that will fetch the employee array and update the table to show all of the data. `NSManagedObjectContext` executes the fetch request that we created using the following code:

```
@fetched_employee = @managed_object_context.
executeFetchRequest(fetch_request,

error: error_pointer)
```

3. Next, we will create the view that will be called when the **+** button is clicked on. Let's create a file named `add_employee_view_controller.rb` and add the following code to it:

```
class AddEmployeeViewController < UIViewController
  attr_accessor :managed_object_context

  def viewDidLoad
    self.view.backgroundColor = UIColor.whiteColor
    self.title = 'Add Employee'
    save_bar_button_item = UIBarButtonItem.alloc.
initWithTitle('Save',
    style: UIBarButtonItemStyleDone,
    target: self,
    action: 'save_employee')
    self.navigationItem.rightBarButtonItem = save_bar_button_item
    load_form
  end

  def save_employee
    # Using Core Data create a new instance of the object employee
    employee = NSEntityDescription.insertNewObjectForEntityForName
(Employee.name,
    inManagedObjectContext: @managed_object_context)
```

```
    # Assign the text of the name text field to the employee
    employee.name = @name.text
    employee.age = @age.text.intValue

    # Create a new pointer for managing the errors
    error_pointer = Pointer.new(:object)

    # Lets persist the new Movie object, saving the managed object
context that contains it
    unless @managed_object_context.save(error_pointer)
      raise "Error saving a new Director: #{error_pointer[0].
description}"
    end

    # Pop the Director View Controller
    self.navigationController.popViewControllerAnimated(true)
  end

  def load_form
    @name = UITextField.alloc.initWithFrame([[50,50],[200,30]])
    @name.borderStyle = UITextBorderStyleRoundedRect
    @name.placeholder = "Name"
    self.view.addSubview(@name)
    @age = UITextField.alloc.initWithFrame([[50,100],[200,30]])
    @age.borderStyle = UITextBorderStyleRoundedRect
    @age.placeholder = "Age"
    self.view.addSubview(@age)
  end
end
```

With the preceding code, we created two text fields, one for name and the
other for age and we first added a **Save** button on top of the view that will
save the employee details by calling the `save_employee` action. In the
`save_employee` action, we used Core Data to create a new instance of the
`employee` object in the following way:

```
employee = NSEntityDescription.insertNewObjectForEntityForName(Emp
loyee.name,

inManagedObjectContext: @managed_object_context)
```

Then, we assigned the value of the text field to the `employee` object and finally saved that object and navigated to `EmployeeViewController`.

4. Let's fire up the terminal and run our application using the following command:

   ```
   $ rake
   ```

   The output is as follows:

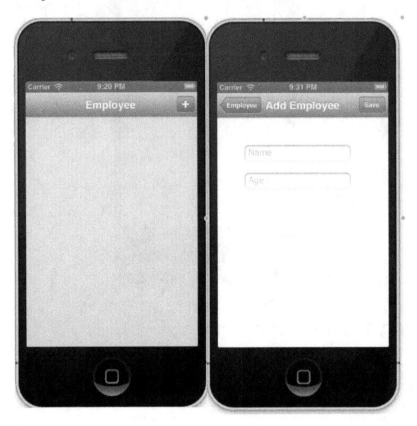

5. Now, let's add data to the **Employee** form using the view:

Deleting the employee

With the completion of the last section, our Core Data application is capable of adding new employee records. But there may be instances when we'll need to delete an employee record. In this section, we'll enhance our app to delete employee records. The use case for this feature will be such that when we slide any row, the system will ask for a confirmation. And once we confirm, the record will be deleted:

1. Update the `employee_view_controller.rb` file with the following code:

```
def tableView(tableView, canEditRowAtIndexPath: indexPath)
   true
 end

def tableView(tableView, commitEditingStyle: editingStyle,
forRowAtIndexPath: indexPath)

   employee = @fetched_employee[indexPath.row]
```

```
    # Ask the NSManagedObjectContext to delete the object
    @managed_object_context.deleteObject(employee)

    # Create a new pointer for managing the errors
    error_pointer = Pointer.new(:object)

    # Lets persist the deleted employee object, saving the managed
object context that contains it
    unless @managed_object_context.save(error_pointer)
      raise "Error deleting an Employee: #{error_pointer[0].
description}"
    end

    # Create a new mutable copy of the fetched_employee array
    mutable_fetched_employee = @fetched_employee.mutableCopy

    # Remove the employee from the array
    mutable_fetched_employee.delete(employee)

    # Assign the modified array to our fetched_employee property
    @fetched_employee = mutable_fetched_employee

    # Tell the table view to delete the row
    tableView.deleteRowsAtIndexPaths([indexPath],
                                  withRowAnimation:UITableViewRo
wAnimationFade)
  end
```

With the iOS `tableView`, we have a direct way of creating or deleting a row. In the preceding code, we first passed the value `true` to the `tableView(tableView, canEditRowAtIndexPath: indexPath)` delegate. Then in order to perform a delete action, we defined the `tableView(tableView, commitEditingStyle: editingStyle, forRowAtIndexPath: indexPath)` delegate.

2. Once we fetch the row that we want to delete, we use `NSManagedObjectContext` to delete that object:

   ```
   @managed_object_context.deleteObject(employee)
   ```

 Remember that we have to always call `save` to persist it to our database.

3. Let's fire up the terminal and run the application using the following command:

```
$rake
```

The output is as follows:

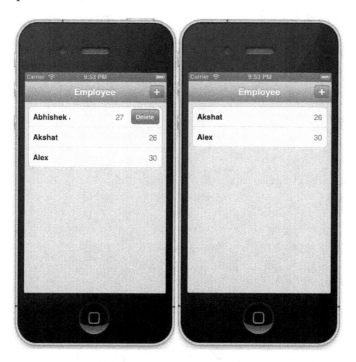

As shown in the preceding screenshot, when we slide the row, we get a system prompt to delete the row. And once we click on **Delete**, the row gets deleted.

Address Book – manage your contacts

Address Book for iOS provides a way to store the contact information and other personal information of people in a centralized database that can then be shared between various applications. In this section, we will perform basic operations related to the Address Book.

We will perform the following operations in this section:

- Access the device's Address Book
- Choose a desired user
- Copy data from the Address Book into our application

Perform the following steps to work with an Address Book:

1. Let's first create a sample address book application with our favorite `motion` command:

   ```
   $motion create AddressBook_example
   ```

2. Next, let's create a controller named `addressbook_controller.rb` and replace the following code in `app_delegate.rb` so that our delegate points to our address book controller:

   ```
   class AppDelegate
     def application(application, didFinishLaunchingWithOptions:launc
   hOptions)

       @window = UIWindow.alloc.initWithFrame(UIScreen.mainScreen.
   bounds)
       @window.rootViewController = AddressbookController.alloc.init
       @window.makeKeyAndVisible


       true
     end
   end
   ```

3. Next, in our `addressbook_controller.rb` controller, which will initially be empty, we will add a button and two labels. With the button, we will access our Address Book and thereafter choose the desired contact. In the labels, we will display the data of the user that we had selected from the Address Book. Let's add the following code in our `addressbook_controller` controller:

   ```
   def viewDidLoad
       view.backgroundColor = UIColor.underPageBackgroundColor
       load_button
       load_labels
   end

   def load_button

       @phonebook_button = UIButton.buttonWithType(UIButtonTypeRou
   ndedRect)
       @phonebook_button.frame = [[50, 20], [200, 50]]
       @phonebook_button.setTitle("Click from Contacts",
   forState:UIControlStateNormal)
         @phonebook_button.addTarget(self, action: :phonebook_
   access, forControlEvents:UIControlEventTouchUpInside)
       view.addSubview(@phonebook_button)
   ```

```
        end


    def load_labels

            @first_name = UILabel.new
            @first_name.text = 'First Name'
            @first_name.frame = [[100,100],[150,50]]

            @phone_number = UILabel.new
            @phone_number.text = 'Phone Number'
            @phone_number.frame = [[100,200],[150,50]]

            view.addSubview(@first_name)
            view.addSubview(@phone_number)

        end
```

4. Let's `rake` and see the progress so far:

    $rake

    The output is as follows:

5. In the preceding step, we mentioned about a `phonebook_access` method; let's create it. This method will help us access our device's Address Book. Further, let's add the following code to our `addressbook_controller.rb` file:

```
def addressbook_access
    @people_picker = ABPeoplePickerNavigationController.alloc.init
    @people_picker.peoplePickerDelegate = self
      presentModalViewController(@people_picker, animated:true)
end
```

6. Once again, let's execute the `rake` command and see if we are able to access the Address Book by clicking on the **Click for contacts** button:

7. With the last step, we are in our Address Book and can see the list of contacts. Next, we need to add a method that will copy the desired contact and navigate back to our application. This can be done with `peoplePickerNavigationController`. Further, we'll add the following code in `addressbook_controller`:

```
def peoplePickerNavigationController(peoplePicker, shouldContinueA
fterSelectingPerson:person)
    self.displayPerson(person)
    self.dismissModalViewControllerAnimated(true)

end
```

8. Now we need to display all of the data we have copied from the Address Book. This can be done using the `displayPerson` method that will let us use the saved values. Add the following method to `addressbook_controller`:

```
def displayPerson(person)
    firstname = ABRecordCopyValue(person,
KABPersonFirstNameProperty)
    phoneNumbers = ABRecordCopyValue(person,
KABPersonPhoneProperty)
    phone = ABMultiValueCopyValueAtIndex(phoneNumbers, 0)
    @phone_number.text = phone
    @first_name.text = firstname

end
```

Great! But we have missed something. What if a user changes his mind and does not want any contact? We need to find a way to get back to the original application from the Address Book. This can be done by adding the following three-line method in `addressbook_controller`:

```
def peoplePickerNavigationControllerDidCancel(peoplePicker)
    self.dismissModalViewControllerAnimated(true)
end
```

Do it yourself

So far we have learned a lot; now let's use our acquired knowledge and improvise our restro application by implementing the following changes:

Task 1 – show nearest restaurant

To get data from the server, use the `http://restro.nalwaya.com/restaurants/find_restaurent_distance.json?latitude=#{latitude}&&longitude=#{longitude}` API.

You have to pass the latitude and longitude with this request, and in return, you will get a list of restaurants in the JSON format. Use this as input and create a view displaying the results.

Task 2 – mark each restaurant on a map with a pin

Use the `http://restro.nalwaya.com/restaurants/search.json?city={city_name}` API that will give you a list of restaurants with their latitude and longitude in the JSON format. Use these coordinates to show their location on the map.

Once you are done with this exercise, compare your solution with the one available in the chapter code available with this book.

Summary

The following is what we have learned in this chapter:

- How to access Camera
- How to use Core Location
- How to use different device gestures
- How to store data on a phone using Core Data
- How to access the Address Book

Now that we are acclimatized with the basics of RubyMotion, in the next chapter we will dig deep into the advanced features of iOS SDK with RubyMotion. iOS SDK is very powerful and has vast functionalities. In the next chapter, we will discuss how to use `.storyboard`, `.xib`, and `WebView` in detail, to create a truly interactive application.

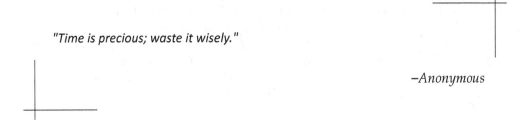

Interface Builder and WebView – More Goodies!

"Time is precious; waste it wisely."

—Anonymous

In this chapter we will learn about some features of iOS development with RubyMotion. Xcode is a very advanced IDE and has many qualities, which we can exploit to develop faster and better iOS applications. In this chapter we will also learn how to use an **Interface Builder** for rapid development with RubyMotion. We will also have a look at some key elements of Xcode, such as `.xib`, `.nib`, and WebView, to create real-life interactive apps.

Interface Builder

Xcode's Interface Builder allows you to create your application's user interface visually, instead of writing code. Interface Builder is a great tool that is very simple to use and is pivotal in making iOS development really fast. Therefore, the Interface Builder used along with RubyMotion further reduces development time. We can say these are two delicious recipes independently, but when used together, it's the ultimate formula to make beautiful iOS apps as quickly as possible.

Interface Builder comes with Xcode. Before we jump into using Interface Builder, it's important to understand that although Interface Builder creates the UI using the drag-and-drop mechanism, it is however not creating the Objective-C code behind the scene. It's creating an XML description of the GUI you're building, and the Cocoa Touch framework uses that XML to actually create the UI elements, such as label and textbox, for your application at runtime. Everything we do in Interface Builder could be done by writing lines of Ruby code—that's exactly what we have been doing from the beginning of this book—but shortly you will see how things get really easy with a GUI builder.

XCode uses XML only for the editing stage, which is then compiled to nibs. Cocoa Touch never sees the XML source.

Before we begin using Interface Builder, let's understand some jargon associated with XCode development. The GUI builder provides options to drag-and-drop buttons, table views, and text fields into your app window. The resulting interface is stored as a .xib file. A .xib file is an XML representation of your objects and their instance variables, and it is compiled into a .nib file when your application is built. The .xib file is easier to work with but the .nib file is smaller and easier to parse, that's why the file that actually ships with your application is a .nib file.

The .nib file is short for NeXT Interface Builder.

Let's try the Interface Builder

So far we have created the views for our **Restro** application views by writing code in Ruby. In this section, let's create a view using the GUI-based Interface Builder. We will create a **Contact Us** form and use it in our application.

The Interface Builder is integrated into Xcode, which is a one stop IDE for any Apple-related development, whether it's for iOS devices or Mac. We will create a `.xib` file and then use this file in our RubyMotion project by performing the following steps:

1. Open Xcode and click on **Create a new Xcode Project**.

2. Click on **Single View Application**, as we need only one `.xib` file.

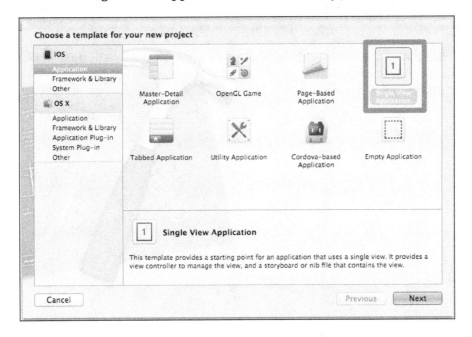

3. Enter this data in the project-creation wizard. Notice that we have selected the device as **iPhone**. We can also see the other options, such as **iPad** and **Universal**. If you want to create a single application to be used on both iPhone and iPad, use the **Universal** option from the drop-down list. Also, unselect the **Use Storyboards** option.

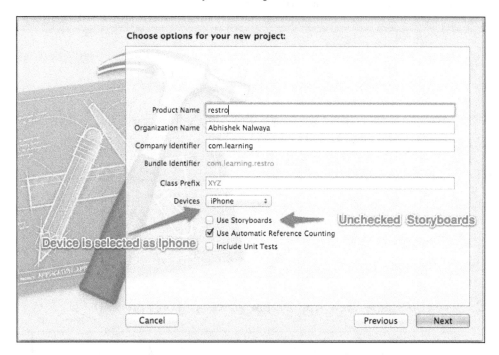

4. Save the project in a folder of your choice; your project will then be loaded in XCode. Click on `ViewController.xib` and you will be able to see the Interface Builder.

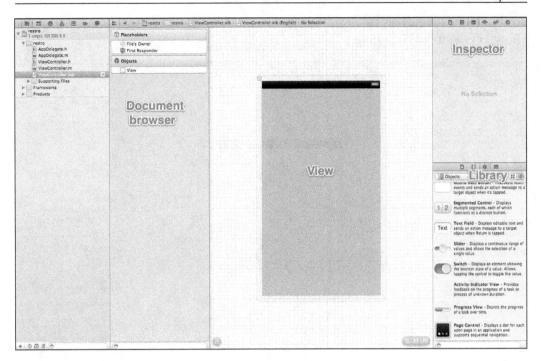

The Interface Builder has a fairly simple layout; it consists of four main windows:

- View
- Library
- Document browser
- Inspector

The View window is where you construct your interface. You will drag-and-drop items from the Library window onto the View window to place them. The document browser allows you to browse hierarchically the elements you have placed in your .nib file. Finally, the Inspector window shows you all of the different attributes of the selected element and allows you to edit them.

And now the magic begins; drag **Navigation Bar** from Library to view the section as shown in the following image:

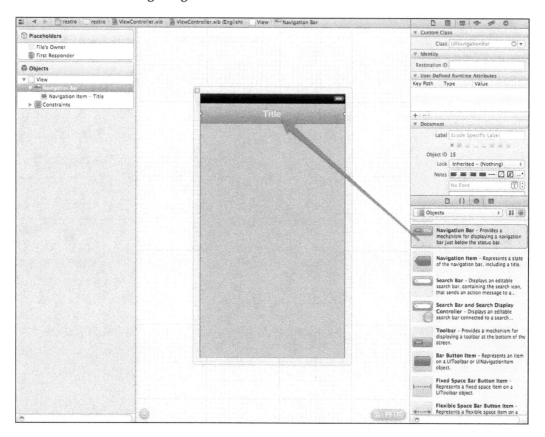

When you select **Navigation Bar**, you will see many properties in the Inspector window. Change the tag value to **1** in the Inspector window. Remember that we will use this tag value in the RubyMotion project code. We need to wire our `View Controller` elements. The easiest way to do this is to use its **Tag** attribute. **Tag** is an `integer` property of the `UIView` class that you can use to identify your views. Basically, you have to set a unique integer for each `UIView` class you need to access from your `UIViewController` element.

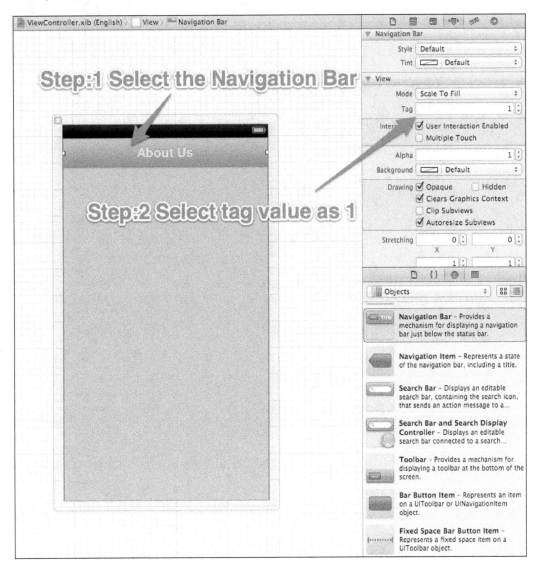

Similarly, add a text field for e-mail and change the value for the placeholder to Email as shown in the following screenshot. There are a lot of properties associated with every Library object; for example, in case of a text field, we have changed the keyboard value to Email as it suits our requirement; but you are free to go ahead and play with other properties too. Using Email will show a keyboard customized for entering e-mail addresses.

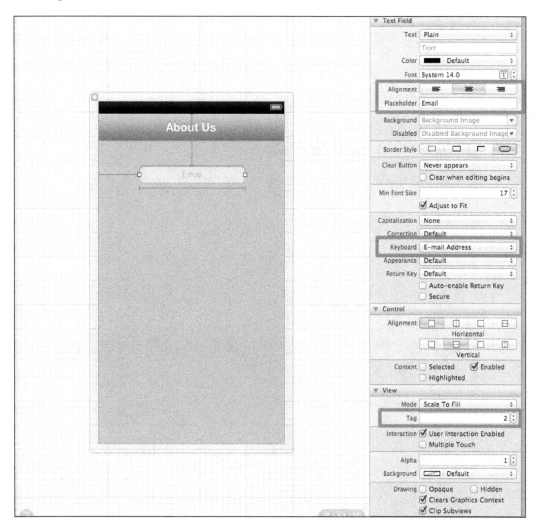

Next, we need a button. Let's drag-and-drop a button onto the View window.

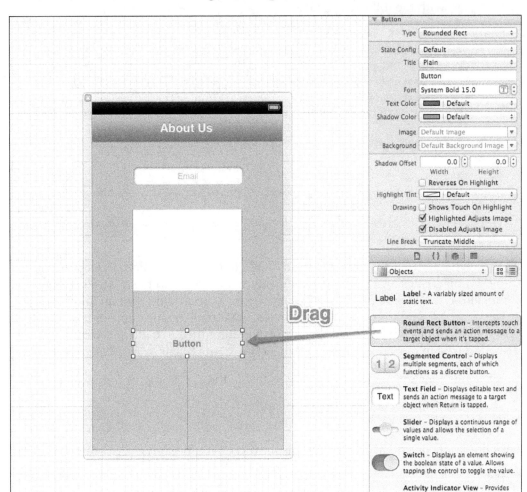

.xib to RubyMotion

In this section, we will import our .xib file into our RubyMotion project. Open the folder of the Xcode project and locate ViewController.xib. It's inside a folder named en.lproj; copy it into the resources folder of your **Restro** application, which we created in the last chapter.

Update the `about_controller.rb file` in the `restro` app, which we created in the last chapter, with the following code:

```
def setupNavigationBar
  back= UIBarButtonItem.alloc.initWithTitle("Back", style:UIBarButtonI
temStylePlain,target:nil ,action:nil)
  self.navigationItem.backBarButtonItem = back;
  contact_us_button = UIBarButtonItem.alloc.initWithTitle("Contact
Us", style:UIBarButtonItemStylePlain ,target:self, action:"contact_
us")
  self.navigationItem.rightBarButtonItem = contact_us_button
end
def contact_us
  contact_us_controller = ContactUsController.alloc.initWithNibName("V
iewController", bundle:nil)
  presentModalViewController(contact_us_controller, animated:true)
end
```

As we have imported the `.xib` file from Xcode to the RubyMotion project, RubyMotion creates a `.nib` file automatically when we build the code with the `Rake` command. Here, we are creating a `View Controller` variable with an initializer `initWithNibName` that receives a parameter, which will be the name of the `.nib` file. This initializer has the responsibility of instantiating the `.nib` file and wiring the `View` declared in the `view` property of the `View Controller variable`.

Create a file `contact_us_controller.rb` inside the app folder as follows:

```
class ContactUsController < UIViewController
end
```

Let's fire up the terminal and run the application with the following command:

$rake

The following screenshot shows the output of the preceding command:

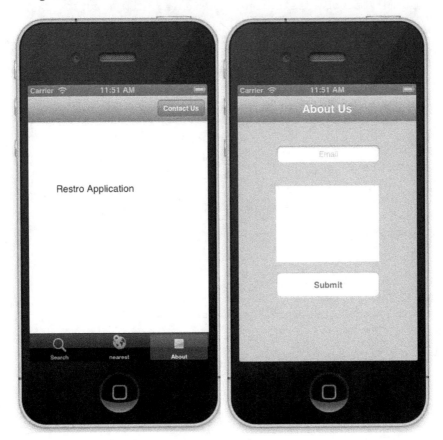

Next, let's update `contact_us_controller.rb` with the following code:

```ruby
class ContactUsController < UIViewController
  HEADER_TAG = 1
  EMAIL_BOX_TAG = 2
  INFORMATION_BOX_TAG = 3
  SUBMIT_BUTTON_TAG = 4
  def viewDidLoad
    @header = self.view.viewWithTag(HEADER_TAG)
    @email_box = self.view.viewWithTag(EMAIL_BOX_TAG)
```

```
    @information_box = self.view.viewWithTag(INFORMATION_BOX_TAG)
    @submit_button = self.view.viewWithTag(SUBMIT_BUTTON_TAG)
    @submit_button.addTarget(self,
           action:"send_message", forControlEvents:UIControlEventTou
chUpInside)
    tapGesture = UITapGestureRecognizer.alloc.initWithTarget(self,
action:"hideKeyboard")
    tapGesture.cancelsTouchesInView = false
    view.addGestureRecognizer(tapGesture)
  end

  def send_message
    if form_valid?
      puts "Submitted the button with correct values"
      close
    else
      puts "Invalid Values"
    end
  end
  def close
    dismissModalViewControllerAnimated true
  end

  #method to hide keyboard when user taps on a scrollview
  def hideKeyboard
    @information_box.resignFirstResponder
end

def form_valid?
  not @email_box.text.empty? and not @information_box.text.empty?
  and not @email_box.text.match(/\A([^@\s]+)@((?:[-a-z0-9]+\.)+[a-z]
{2,})\Z/i).nil?
  end
end
```

Let's start the application by using the following command:

$rake

Enter a few incorrect values in the form and you will get **Invalid value** printed on the terminal. Once you enter the values correctly in the form and submit it, it will be pulled down.

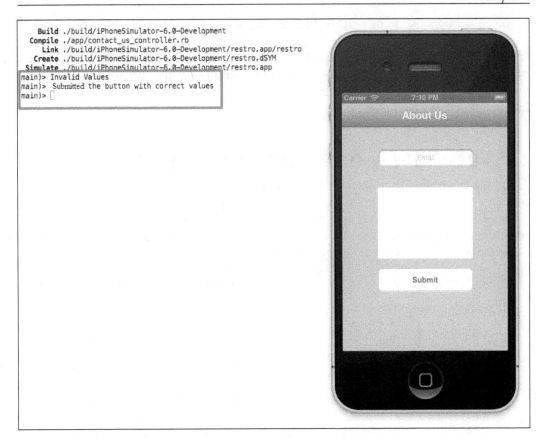

Now let's understand the code. First we have assigned the tags to the attributes that we had created in Interface Builder. And then we have used these tags to wire our variables to those components.

`self.view.viewWithTag(HEADER_TAG)`

The preceding command will retrieve a subview of `self.view` based on its tag.

We have also created an `action` item for the **Submit** button. That means when we click on the **Submit** button, it will call the action `send_message`.

```
    @submit_button.addTarget(self,
        action:"send_message", forControlEvents:UIControlEventTouchUpIn
side)
```

In the `send_message` action, we are checking whether the form is valid or not.

Some developers like to design the user interface using Interface Builder; others prefer to work entirely with code. One of the reasons is that when connecting Interface Builder outlets and actions to your code, it is easy to make a mistake. This often results in an error that is more difficult to debug than if you had simply written the entire code, as you have to debug in two places (Interface Builder and your code) instead of just one (the code).

UIWebView – embed web content

There is a possibility that we have to show web content in our application. The `UIWebView` class helps us to do exactly that. To do this, simply create a `UIWebView` object, attach it to a window, and send a request to load web content. We can also use this class to move back and forth in the history of web pages and you can even set some web content properties programmatically.

Now let's create a `UIWebView` class that displays www.rubymotion.com in our view.

Update `about_controller.rb` with the following code:

```
def submit_button
  @visitButton = UIButton.buttonWithType(UIButtonTypeRoundedRect)
  @visitButton.frame = [[80,10],[180,37]]
  @visitButton.setTitle("Visit", forState:UIControlStateNormal)
  @visitButton.setTitle("You have clicked me", forState:UIControlStat
eHighlighted)
  @visitButton.addTarget(self, action:"load_some_view", forControlEven
ts:UIControlEventTouchDown)
  view.addSubview(@visitButton)
end
def load_some_view
      @my_web_view = UIWebView.alloc.
initWithFrame([[0,100],[320,220]])
      @my_web_view.delegate = self
      @my_web_view.scalesPageToFit = "YES"
      view.addSubview(@my_web_view)
      url = NSURL.URLWithString("http://www.rubymotion.com")
      request = NSURLRequest.requestWithURL(url)
      @my_web_view.loadRequest(request)
end
```

Now let's understand the code. Take the following line:

```
url = NSURL.URLWithString("http://www.rubymotion.com")
```

Here, NSURL.URLWithString tells our application that the text passed is a web address or a URL, which is now an NSURL object called url.

```
request = NSURLRequest.requestWithURL(url)
```

NSURLRequest.requestWithURL processes the url variable passed as a request. It is now a request object called request.

```
@my_web_view.loadRequest(request)
```

Finally, we load the request into the WebView class, which we have named @my_web_view.

Let's fire up the terminal and run our application as follows to see the results:

$rake

The following screenshot shows the output of the preceding command:

Summary

Let's recap what we have learned in this chapter:

- Xcode Interface Builder with RubyMotion
- Using WebView to embed web content in your application with RubyMotion

In the next chapter we will focus on a pivotal part of the software development lifecycle, which is testing. We will learn how to write test cases for the RubyMotion project and test our application on iOS devices.

Testing – Let's Fail Gracefully

8

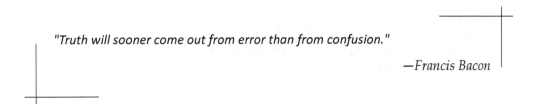

"Truth will sooner come out from error than from confusion."

—*Francis Bacon*

In order to maintain high quality of a software product, testing is a very important part of the software development life cycle. In this chapter we will learn how we can test RubyMotion applications. We will learn to write unit tests, which can test an isolated code, and then learn functional testing, which will help us automate the UI tests. The following topics will be covered in this chapter:

- Unit testing
- Functional testing
- Device events

Unit testing

The goal of unit testing is to isolate each part of the program and show that the individual parts function properly. RubyMotion uses MacBacon, which is an iOS flavor of Bacon.

Bacon is a smaller clone of RSpec. With less than 350 LOCs, we nevertheless get all the essential features.

Here, we will also follow **Test Driven Development** (TDD), a way of working where unit tests are created before the code itself is written. Of course, the tests will fail initially because we don't have anything. That's the philosophy of TDD; first we write the test case, it fails, we then refractor our code and once again write the feature code, and this time our test cases pass and the code is considered complete.

The idea here is that the developer himself wears the hat of a tester. We first document the feature in the form of a test, which fails, then we write our code and refractor, and once again document with a test case for the next feature.

First, let's create an application, which we will be using to learn how to write test cases for use with TDD.

```
$motion create LearnTest
```

In the folder structure, we can see a spec folder and a file main_spec.rb placed inside this folder. This is the default test file generated by the RubyMotion generator; this is where we write our test cases.

Let's write our first test case in the main_spec.rb file inside the spec folder as follows:

```
describe "Application 'LearnTest'" do
  before do
    @app = UIApplication.sharedApplication
  end

  it "has one window" do
    @app.windows.size.should == 1
  end
end
```

Bacon gives you a way to encapsulate what you're testing via the describe block. As the name suggests, the describe block is used to describe the behavior of a class as follows:

```
describe "Application 'LearnTest'" do
end
```

Tests are written using the it block. The test has a window, which checks if our application has a window as follows:

```
it "has one window" do
  @app.windows.size.should == 1
end
```

As you can see, the syntax of these tests is very readable and you can easily understand what it means. In this case, `@app.windows.size.should == 1` means that your application should have one window.

The `describe()` method clasps into the Bacon API and gives us the `Spec::ExampleGroup` class. As the name suggests, it is a group of examples. These examples are actually the expected behavior of the object. If you're familiar with the xUnit tools such as `Test::Unit`, you can think of an `ExampleGroup` class as being akin to a test case.

Let's run the test case with the following commands:

```
$ rake spec
Build ./build/iPhoneSimulator-6.0-Development
  Compile ./app/app_delegate.rb
  Compile /Library/RubyMotion/lib/motion/spec.rb
  Compile /Library/RubyMotion/lib/motion/spec/helpers/ui.rb
  Compile ./spec/main_spec.rb
    Create ./build/iPhoneSimulator-6.0-Development/LearnTest_spec.app
      Link ./build/iPhoneSimulator-6.0-Development/LearnTest_spec.app/
LearnTest
    Create ./build/iPhoneSimulator-6.0-Development/LearnTest_spec.app/Info.
plist
    Create ./build/iPhoneSimulator-6.0-Development/LearnTest_spec.app/
PkgInfo
    Create ./build/iPhoneSimulator-6.0-Development/LearnTest_spec.dSYM
    Simulate ./build/iPhoneSimulator-6.0-Development/LearnTest_spec.app
Application 'LearnTest'
  has one window [FAILED]

Bacon::Error: 0.==(1) failed
  spec.rb:649:in 'satisfy:': Application 'LearnTest' - has one window
  spec.rb:663:in 'method_missing:'
  spec.rb:279:in 'block in run_spec_block'
  spec.rb:403:in 'execute_block'
  spec.rb:279:in 'run_spec_block'
  spec.rb:294:in 'run'

1 specifications (1 requirements), 1 failures, 0 errors
```

We can see that one test failed (`Bacon::Error: 0.==(1)`). That is exactly what we wanted.

This means that `@app.windows.size` should expect the value as 1 but the actual value right now is 0. This is because till now we have not created a window in our application.

Next, let's write the code to create a window and update the `app_delegate.rb` file with the following code:

```
class AppDelegate
  def application(application, didFinishLaunchingWithOptions:launchOp
tions)
    @window = UIWindow.alloc.initWithFrame(UIScreen.mainScreen.
applicationFrame)
    @window.makeKeyAndVisible
  true
  end
end
```

Let's run the `specs` file as follows:

```
$rake spec
Application 'LearnTest'
  - has one window


1 specifications (1 requirements), 0 failures, 0 errors
```

We see that our test has passed and the code is therefore complete; mission accomplished!

The following are some commonly used assertions with MacBacon:

- `should.` and `should.be`
- `should.equal`
- `should.match`
- `should.be.identical_to`/`should.be.same_as`
- `should.raise(*exceptions) { }`
- `should.change { }`
- `should.throw(symbol) { }`
- `should.satisfy { |object| }`

Now let's create one more test by adding the following code to your
`main_spec.rb` file:

```
it "should set rootviewcontroller as RootViewController" do
    @app.keyWindow.rootViewController.class.should ==
RootViewController
end
```

This test checks whether we have the `rootViewController` property in our
application whose name should be `RootViewController`. Run this test case
and it should fail, as we have not yet created `RootViewController`.

Let's create a file `root_view_controller.rb` in the app folder as follows:

```
class RootViewController   < UIViewController
def viewDidLoad


      end
end
```

Also update the `app_delegate.rb` file by adding the following line:

```
@window.rootViewController = RootViewController.alloc.init
```

Now when we run the `specs file`, we will find that all the test cases are passed.

Next, let's add some functionality to our application. How about we calculate the
sum of the squares of numbers? Let's first write the tests for this.

Add the following `specs` code to the `main_spec.rb` file in the `spec` folder:

```
describe "sum_of_square_number" do
  it "should return sum of squares of numbers" do
    array = [2,4,1]
    controller.sum_of_square_number(array).should.equal 21
  end

  it "should return 0 if array is blank" do
    array = []
    controller.sum_of_square_number(array).should.equal 0
  end
end
```

When we run the test, they will surely fail, as we have not yet created the `sum_of_square_number` method. So let's create this method and its logic so that our `specs` tests pass, update the `root_view_controller.rb` file, and add the following method:

```
def sum_of_square_number(array)
  sum = 0
  array.each do |number|
    sum = sum + number*number
  end
  sum
end
```

This time, when we run our `specs` tests they will pass.

So far we have learned about testing a piece of code, but it is equally important that we test the user interface, so in the next section we will write a functional test.

 You can create multiple files in your `spec` folder. RubyMotion automatically runs all the files with the `.rb` extension. You can also run individual files even from different locations with the following command:

rake spec files=foo_spec,spec/bar_spec.rb

Functional testing

RubyMotion lets us write functional tests for our controllers and interacts with its views through a set of high-level event generating APIs, by leveraging the functionality of Apple's `UIAutomation` framework without forcing us to write the tests in JavaScript.

Let's now write tests for user interface of the same application. In the following test case, we will test whether we have a label and a button on the screen.

Create the `spec` file `restro_view_controller_spec.rb` in the spec folder:

```
it "should have a label and a button" do
  view('Click Button').should.not.equal nil
  button = view('Click Me')
  button.should.not.equal nil
  button.isEnabled.should.equal true
end
```

The `view(label)` property returns the view that matches the specified accessibility label. The `view` command traverses down through the view hierarchy, starting from the current window. If no view matches our condition, it keeps retrying it until the timeout, which defaults to three seconds. This means you don't need to worry about whether or not the view you're looking for is still being loaded or animated.

Finally, if the timeout passes and no view matches, an exception will be raised.

The default timeout value can be changed through the `Bacon::Functional.default_timeout` property.

 You can also check what buttons are available on view with the classname as follows:

```
views(UIButton) # => [button1, button2]
```

Now to pass this test, let's write the code for this functionality and update the file `root_view_controller.rb` with the following code:

```ruby
def viewDidLoad
  super
  view.backgroundColor = UIColor.whiteColor
  @label = UILabel.new
  @label.text = 'Click Button'
  @label.textAlignment = UITextAlignmentCenter
  @label.frame = [[80,50],[150,50]]
  view.addSubview(@label)
  @normal_button = UIButton.buttonWithType(UIButtonTypeRoundedRect)
  @normal_button.frame = [[80,150],[180,37]]
  @normal_button.setTitle("Click Me", forState:UIControlStateNormal)
  @normal_button.addTarget(self, action:'buttonIsPressed', forControlE
vents:UIControlEventTouchDown)
  view.addSubview(@normal_button)
end
```

Let's fire up the terminal and run the application with the following command:

$rake

The following screenshot shows the output of the preceding command:

We have created a label and a button in this View and now, when we run our spec test, it passes. Next, we want to calculate the sum of the squares of the first 5 numbers on click of a button. Let's first write the spec code for this functionality. Update the file restro_view_controller_spec.rb with the following code:

```
it "should show sum of squares on click of button" do
  tap 'Click Me'
  view('55').should.not.equal nil
end
```

The tap command clicks on the button with the label **Click Me**. There are many options available with the tap command. We will know more about them as we proceed with this chapter.

Now let's write the corresponding code for this `spec` test and update the file `root_view_controller.rb` with the following code:

```
def buttonIsPressed
  array = [1,2,3,4,5]
  @label.text = sum_of_square_number(array).to_s
end
```

Let's fire up the terminal and test our application with the following command:

$rake

The following screenshot shows the output of the preceding command:

We are now familiar with the basic functioning of testing. Next, we will learn how to test the device events with RubyMotion.

Device events

Most of the iOS applications make use of the various device capabilities. As a good practice, we must test these features to deliver high quality apps. RubyMotion gives us an environment to test some device capabilities. Let's discuss a few of them in this section.

Rotate device

We can test the rotation of the device by calling the following event:

```
rotate_device(:to => orientation, :button => location)
```

The `rotate_device` command allows us to pass the following two arguments:

- `to`: This passes the orientation to rotate the device; it can either have portrait or landscape as a value.
- `button`: The `button` here indicates the position of the **home** button; it makes sense if we pass the values based on the first value of orientation. In portrait mode, we can opt for the `:bottom` or `:top` `button` location. In landscape mode, we can opt for `:left` or `:right` with respect to the button location, for example, `rotate_device :to =>` `:portrait, :button =>` `:bottom`.

This device event will rotate the device to the portrait orientation with the **home** button at the bottom.

Now let's use this rotation in our sample application from the previous section. We want to ensure that our application only works in portrait mode. For this we must disable the landscape mode. Let's add a test case for this scenario. Add the following code in the file `root_view_controller_spec.rb`:

```
it "has default orientations for portrait" do
    rotate_device :to => :landscape
    controller.interfaceOrientation.should ==
UIInterfaceOrientationPortrait

    rotate_device :to => :portrait
    controller.interfaceOrientation.should ==
UIInterfaceOrientationPortrait
end
```

With the preceding test case, we rotate the device first in landscape mode and then in portrait mode, and then we test that each rotation is actually in portrait mode.

Let's fire up the terminal and run the test as follows:

```
$rake spec
Application 'LearnTest'
    has one window
    should set rootviewcontroller as RootViewController
```

```
RootViewController
    should have label and button
    should show sum of square on click of button
    has default orientations for portrait [FAILED]

sum_of_square_number
    should written sum of square of numbers
    should written 0 if array is blank

Bacon::Error: 4.==(1) failed
  spec.rb:649:in 'satisfy:': RootViewController - has default
orientations for portrait
  spec.rb:663:in 'method_missing:'
  spec.rb:279:in 'block in run_spec_block'
  spec.rb:403:in 'execute_block'
  spec.rb:279:in 'run_spec_block'
  spec.rb:294:in 'run'
```

As expected, it failed. Let's write its corresponding code to make our app work only in portrait mode.

Update `Rakefile` with the following line of code:

```
app.interface_orientations = [:portrait]
```

Let's test our `spec` file once again and check the output on the console:

```
$rake spec

Application 'LearnTest'
  - has one window
  - should set rootviewcontroller as RootViewController

RootViewController
  - should have label and button
  - should show sum of square on click of button
  - has default orientations for portrait

sum_of_square_number
  - should written sum of square of numbers
  - should written 0 if array is blank


7 specifications (10 requirements), 0 failures, 0 errors
```

All tests passed as expected. Now, let's run the application in a simulator with the following command:

`$rake`

Rotate the device by selecting **Hardware | Rotate Left** in the simulator menu as shown in the following screenshot:

You can see that even after rotation, the interface orientation does not change as shown in the following screenshot:

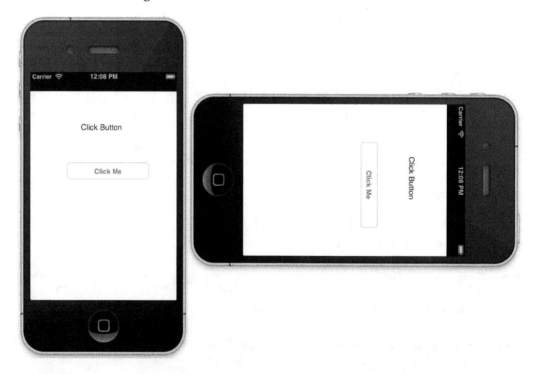

Accelerometer device event

Accelerometer allows us to measure the linear acceleration of the device for your application. We can test the accelerometer features either on a device or with the following `accelerate` event:

```
accelerate(:x => x_axis_acceleration, :y => y_axis_acceleration,
          :z => z_axis_acceleration, :duration => duration)
```

The following parameters can be passed with `accelerate`:

- x: If you hold your device in the portrait orientation and the screen is facing you, the x axis will run from left to right, with values on the left as negative and values on the right as positive.

- y: If you hold your device in the portrait orientation and the screen is facing you, the y axis will run from bottom to top, with values on the bottom as negative and values on the top as positive.

- z: If you hold your device in the portrait orientation and the screen is facing you, the z axis will run from back to front, with values at the back as negative and values towards the front as positive. For example, accelerate: x => 0, :y => 0, :z => -1.

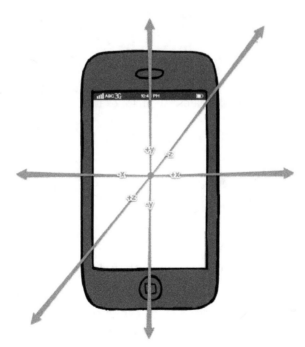

This test case event simulates a device lying on its back.

To trigger a shake motion event, we can use the following method: `shake()`

Gestures

A user of an iOS application uses the app in a number of ways, by tapping or touching the screen and pinching or rotating. With RubyMotion, we can test most of these gestures; let's discuss a few of them in this section.

Most of the gestures operate on views. We can specify the location of our event on the view by either using CGPoint or with the following constants:

- `:top`
- `:top_left`
- `:top_right`
- `:bottom_right`
- `:bottom`
- `:bottom_left`
- `:left`
- `:right`

 CGPoint lets us access a structure that contains a point in a two-dimensional coordinate system, for example, CGPoint.new(100, 200).

Tap

To simulate a tapping event on a view, we can specify a label or a view, and some specific properties as follows:

```
tap(label_or_view, :at => location, :times => number_of_taps, :touches
=> number_of_fingers)
```

Let's understand what the purpose of the optional parameters is:

- `at`: We can specify the location on the view where we want the tap to simulate; the default location is the center of the view.
- `times`: This specifies the number of times to tap the view. The default is a single tap.

- **touches**: iPhone and iPad are multitouch devices; many apps exploit this feature of the iOS devices. You can specify the number of fingers that will be used to tap the view. The default is a single touch.

The following example will tap `Test Label` with the default setting of tapping a view once with a single touch:

```
tap "Test Label"
```

In the next example, we will test the view labeled `Test Label` by tapping five times with two fingers:

```
tap 'Test Label', :times => 5, :touches => 2
```

Flick

Flick generates a sharp moment of the drag gesture as follows:

```
flick(label_or_view, :from => location, :to => location, :duration =>
duration)
```

We can pass the following options with the `flick` method:

- **from**: Specifies the location on the view to start the drag gesture.
- **to**: Specifies the location on the view to end the drag gesture.

The following example generates a flick gesture to the right of the view:

```
flick "test label", :to => :right
```

Pinch open

Pinch open is a gesture using two fingers, which is generally used for zooming the images. With the following method we can generate a pinch open gesture:

```
pinch_open(label_or_view, :from => location, :to => location,
:duration => duration)
```

We can pass the following options with the `pinch_open` method:

`from`: This denotes the starting point for two fingers to begin the pinch open gesture; by default, it is to the left of the view.

`to`: This denotes the ending point for two fingers to finish the pinch open gesture; it defaults to the right.

The following example zooms in on the content view of a `UIScrollView` class:

```
view('Test Zoom').zoomScale # => 1.0
pinch_open 'Test Zoom'
view('Test Zoom').zoomScale # => 2.0
```

Pinch close

Pinch close is a gesture using two fingers, which is generally used for zooming out on images. With the following method we can generate a pinch close gesture:

```
pinch_close(label_or_view, :from => location, :to => location,
:duration => duration)
```

We can pass the following options with the `pinch_close` method:

- `from`: This denotes the starting point for two fingers to begin the pinch close gesture; by default, it is to the right of the view.
- `to`: This denotes the ending point for two fingers to finish the pinch close gesture; by default, it is to the left of the view.

The following example zooms out of the content view of a `UIScrollView` class:

```
view('Test Zoom').zoomScale # => 1.0
pinch_close 'Test Zoom'
view('Test Zoom').zoomScale # => 0.5
```

Drag

A drag gesture is generally used for panning and scrolling; it always has a start and end point. With the following method we can generate a drag gesture:

```
drag(label_or_view, :from => location, :to => location, :number_of_
points => steps,
      :points => path, :touches => number_of_fingers, :duration =>
duration)
```

We can pass the following options with the `drag` method:

- `from`: This denotes the part of the view where the drag gesture will begin. If not specified, it defaults to none.
- `to`: This denotes the part of the view where the drag gesture will end. If not specified, it defaults to none.
- `number_of_points`: The number of points between `:from` and `:to`. It defaults to 20.

- `points`: An array of CGPoint instances that specifies the drag path.
- `touches`: The number of fingers to be used to drag. It defaults to a single touch.

Keep in mind that scrolling in a direction means dragging in the opposite direction.

The following code will scroll down in a scroll view:

```
view('Some Scrollable scrollview').contentOffset.y # => 0
drag 'Some Scrollable scrollview', :from => :bottom
view('Some Scrollable scrollview').contentOffset.y # => 400
```

Rotation

To test the clockwise and anticlockwise rotation gesture, the following method is used. This method will simulate the rotation gesture around the center point of the view.

```
rotate(label_or_view, :radians => angle, :degrees => angle, :touches
=> number_of_fingers, :duration => duration)
```

We can pass the following options with the `rotate` method:

- `radians`: The angle of rotation in radians. It defaults to π.
- `degrees`: The angle of rotation in degrees. It defaults to 180.
- `touches`: The number of fingers used to rotate. It defaults to 2.

Summary

Let's recap all that we have learned in this chapter:

- Unit test cases
- Functional test cases
- How to test device events

So far we have covered the basics and advanced topics related to RubyMotion. And now we are ready to do some fun stuff. In the next chapter we will learn to create games with RubyMotion. Gaming apps are one of (if not the) most popular genres of apps on the App Store. Most of us pass the time playing games on our iOS devices, so why not learn how to use RubyMotion to create our own game. In the next chapter we will learn how to create a game using RubyMotion.

9
Creating a Game

Apple App Store has a wide variety of applications. There are many popular genres of applications available, such as productivity, business, entertainment, and many more. But out of these, the most popular kind are the gaming apps, and to make one yourself is much more exciting. Gaming on iOS devices is a gigantic topic; in this chapter we will cover some basics for creating an engaging gaming app. We will also use a popular library, so that by the end of this iteration, we will be able to make a simple and fun gaming application. The following topics will be covered in this chapter:

- Cocos2D
- Understanding gaming basics by creating a game app

Cocos2D

Cocos2D is a powerful library for game development, which saves a lot of time by handling trivial things while building your game. Common things that are regularly needed for game development, such as direction, sprite, cool graphical effects, animations, physics libraries, sound engines, and a lot more are already provided by libraries and APIs.

Cocos2D organizes game development like the making of a movie where you are made to sit in the director's chair. For example, you will have a scene for the startup menu of the game, another for the main game, and then another for the game over scene with options that concludes the playing episode. You have to literally use the `Director` class to create a director object, which drives the whole application forward.

All the basic tasks, such as starting the game, pausing the game, and creating various scenes are handled by Cocos2D.

Inside the scenes, you can have a number of layers that contain nodes such as sprites, labels, menus, and more. These nodes can contain other nodes as well. This can be nicely demonstrated with the help of the following figure:

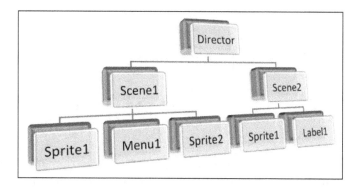

Let's create a game – Whac-A-Mole

We will create an iPhone version of the popular arcade game *Whac-A-Mole*. When the game starts, moles (an animal) will begin to pop up from the bottom of the screen. The objective of the game is to hit the mole, thereby adding to the player's score:

1. Create an application using the following command:

   ```
   motion create GameApp
   ```

2. Now, as we are using an external library for our application, let's first install CocoaPods. Run the following commands on your terminal:

   ```
   $ sudo gem install cocoapods
   $ pod setup
   $ sudo gem install motion-cocoapods
   ```

3. Update the Rakefile:

   ```
   $:.unshift("/Library/RubyMotion/lib")
   require 'motion/project'
   require 'motion-cocoapods'

   Motion::Project::App.setup do |app|
     # Use 'rake config' to see complete project settings.
     app.name = 'GameApp'
     app.pods do
       pod 'cocos2d'
     end
   end
   ```

Now we are all set to begin coding for our app.

Let's start coding!

As in Cocos2D, we need to create a director for starting the game. Let's create one:

1. Update the `app_delegate.rb` file with the following code:

```
class AppDelegate
  def application(application, didFinishLaunchingWithOptions:launc
hOptions)

    # Create a window to present our director
    @window = UIWindow.alloc.initWithFrame(UIScreen.mainScreen.
bounds)

    # Create CCGLView view that will be used by the director to
present the game scenes

    game_view = CCGLView.viewWithFrame(@window.bounds,
pixelFormat: KEAGLColorFormatRGBA8, depthFormat: 0,
preserveBackbuffer: false, sharegroup: nil, multiSampling: false,
numberOfSamples: 0)



    # Create Director shared instance
    @director = CCDirector.sharedDirector
    @director.wantsFullScreenLayout = true
    @director.animationInterval = 1.0/60

    # Assign the view used for the director to present the game
scenes
    @director.view = game_view


    # Create a navigation controller to store our game director
and assign the navigation controller to the window
    @navigation_controller = UINavigationController.alloc.
initWithRootViewController(@director)
    @navigation_controller.navigationBarHidden = true
    @window.rootViewController = @navigation_controller
    @window.makeKeyAndVisible


    # Configuration for our game images, this is very helpful when
you want to use compressed images or those with a different
    # pixel format
```

```
    CCTexture2D.defaultAlphaPixelFormat = KCCTexture2DPixelFormat_
RGBA8888
    CCTexture2D.PVRImagesHavePremultipliedAlpha(true)

    # Configuration for the names of the images that will be used
on the game
    file_utils = CCFileUtils.sharedFileUtils
    file_utils.enableFallbackSuffixes = false
    true
  end

end
```

2. Then run the application with the `rake` command:

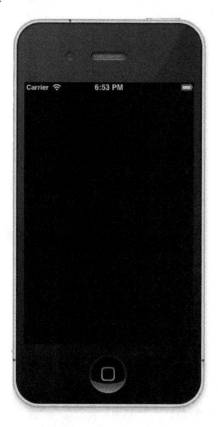

Let's understand what we have done so far.

First, we created a window and a view:

```
@window = UIWindow.alloc.initWithFrame(UIScreen.mainScreen.bounds)
game_view = CCGLView.viewWithFrame(@window.bounds,
                            pixelFormat: KEAGLColorFormatRGBA8,
                            depthFormat: 0,
                            preserveBackbuffer: false,
                            sharegroup: nil,
                            multiSampling: false,
                            numberOfSamples: 0)
```

You must have noted that we used the `CCGLView` class to create a view, which is available with Cocos2D. It is inherited from `EAGLview`, which is in turn a subclass of the `UIView` subclass that renders the `OpenGL` scene.

After this, we defined an object for the `CCDirector` class that creates and handles the main window and manages how and when to execute the scenes. It initializes the `OpenGL ES` context. The `CCDirector` class starts or pauses the game; it also handles when a phone call or text message comes in, so that it can automatically pause the game. We have also set the view to the `CCDirector` object.

```
@director = CCDirector.sharedDirector
@director.wantsFullScreenLayout = true
@director.animationInterval = 1.0/60
@director.view = game_view
```

Now let's create a scene, which will be inherited by `CCScene`:

1. Create a file named `game_scene.rb`:

```
class GameScene < CCScene
  def init
    if super
    end
    self
  end

end
```

2. Add the following code in the `app_delegate.rb` file:

```
@director.pushScene(GameScene.node)
```

Basically, it will tell the `@director` object to open `GameScene` once the application loads.

3. Now, as we have created a blank scene, let's start adding graphical layers to our game. Create a file named `background_layer.rb` and update the following code:

```
class BackgroundLayer < CCLayer
  def init
    if super
      label = CCLabelTTF.labelWithString('We are creating a game',
                                          fontName:'Marker Felt',
                                          fontSize:24)

      window_size = CCDirector.sharedDirector.winSize
      label.position = CGPointMake(window_size.width / 2, window_
size.height / 2)
      self.addChild(label)
    end
    self
  end
end
```

The `CCLabelTTF` class is used to display text on the scene. We can also pass `fontName` and `fontSize` while initiating the label. Then we have to assign the positions to the label.

> The `CCDirector` class also provides the height and width of the screen with the following command:
>
> **CCDirector.sharedDirector.winSize**

4. Now, to add this layer to our scene, update the `game_scene.rb` file with the following code:

```
class GameScene < CCScene

  def init
    if super
      background_layer = BackgroundLayer.node
      # Add it to the scene
      self.addChild(background_layer)
    end
    self
  end

end
```

5. Now let's run the application to check our progress so far:

We can see the text displayed on the screen. This is some test text that we have added, so why not replace this text with a background image.

 You can download the image provided in the resource folder from the exercise code, which is provided with the book.

6. To display a background image, update the `background_layer.rb` file with the following code:

```ruby
class BackgroundLayer < CCLayer

  def init
    if super

      background_sprite = CCSprite.spriteWithFile('sky.png')
      # We need to get the screen size for positioning the sprite
```

```
      screen_size = CCDirector.sharedDirector.winSize

      # We need to get the screen size for positioning the sprite
      background_sprite.position = CGPointMake(screen_size.width /
2, screen_size.height / 2)

    # Setting the position for image
    self.addChild(background_sprite)
  end

  self
end

end
```

We have created a CCSprite object, which is loaded from an image named
sky.png.

7. Now run the application using the rake command:

8. Now, as our game has a lot of objects, we have to design it for the landscape mode, so that the users can interact with the game comfortably. For that, open the `Rake` file and add `app.interface_orientations = [:landscape_left]` in this file, and run the application using the `rake` command:

9. That's cool! Let's now add grass in the game layer. Create a file named `game_layer.rb` and add the following code:

```ruby
class GameLayer < CCLayer

  def init

    if super
      # We need to get the screen size for positioning the sprite
      screen_size = CCDirector.sharedDirector.winSize
      @grass = CCSprite.spriteWithFile('Grass.png')
      @grass.position = CGPointMake(screen_size.width / 2, screen_size.height / 12)

      # Add the sprite to the Layer
      self.addChild(@grass)
    end
    self
  end
end
```

10. Then add this layer in our scene and update `game_scene.rb` with the following code:

```
game_layer = GameLayer.node
  self.addChild(game_layer)
```

11. Let's start the application and see what we have done:

12. Wow! We can see green grass. Next, let's add three mole animals to our view by updating the `game_layer.rb` file with the following code:

```
class GameLayer < CCLayer

  def init
    if super
      # We need to get the screen size for positioning the sprite
      screen_size = CCDirector.sharedDirector.winSize
      @grass = CCSprite.spriteWithFile('Grass.png')

      @grass.position = CGPointMake(screen_size.width / 2, screen_size.height / 12)
      # Add the sprite to the Layer
      self.addChild(@grass)


      @mole = []

      # Create a new sprite instance for drawing our mole
      @mole1 = CCSprite.spriteWithFile('mole.png')

      @mole1.position = CGPointMake(screen_size.width / 2, 0)
```

```
        # Add the sprite to the Layer
        self.addChild(@mole1, z: 0)
        # We need to get the screen size for positioning the
    sprite
        screen_size = CCDirector.sharedDirector.winSize

        @mole2 = CCSprite.spriteWithFile('mole.png')
        @mole2.position = CGPointMake(screen_size.width / 4, 0)
        self.addChild(@mole2)

        @mole3= CCSprite.spriteWithFile('mole.png')
        @mole3.position = CGPointMake(3* screen_size.width / 4, 0)
        self.addChild(@mole3)

        @moles = [@mole1, @mole2, @mole3]

      end
      self
    end
  end
```

13. And now run the application:

Wow! We can see three moles at the bottom of the page. Let's add some motion to these moles.

Adding motion to moles

To make things more interesting, we want these moles to be moving up and down—this will add a challenge for the app users:

1. Update the `game_layer.rb` file by adding the following method to it:

```
def popMole(mole)
    moveUp = CCMoveBy.actionWithDuration(0.2, position:
CGPointMake(0, mole.contentSize.height));
    easeMoveUp = CCEaseInOut.actionWithAction(moveUp, rate:
3.0);
    easeMoveDown = easeMoveUp.reverse
    delay = CCDelayTime.actionWithDuration(0.5)
    mole.runAction(CCSequence.actionsWithArray([easeMoveUp,
delay, easeMoveDown]));
end
```

`CCMoveBy` moves the mole up along the Y axis according to the height of the mole. To make the movement look more natural, we have used the `CCEaseInOut` class. To make the mole move back down again, we have used the `reverse` action. The `reverse` method on an action pulls the object in the opposite direction. We have then created an action to pause the popping action of the moles using the `CCDelayTime` class.

Now, we have combined all the actions into a sequence using the `CCSequence` class. The `CCSequence` class allows us to chain together a sequence of actions that are performed in order, one at a time.

2. As we have three moles, let's call this motion randomly for each mole. We'll also update the `game_layer.rb` file by adding the following method to it:

```
def popAnyMole
    random = Random.new
    @moles.each do |mole|

        if (random.rand(1..100) % 3 == 0)
            if (@mole1.numberOfRunningActions == 0 and @mole2.
numberOfRunningActions==0 and  @mole3.numberOfRunningActions==0 )
                popMole(mole)
            end
        end
    end
end
```

3. We just need one more thing before we are ready to roll. We need to schedule this method to run as often as possible by adding the following line of code to the `init` method of the `game_layer.rb` file:

```
schedule :popAnyMole
```

4. Now run the application:

We can see that the mole is randomly popping up and down.

5. Let's now make this mole hide behind the grass. To do so, update the `game_layer.rb` file and modify the `init` method by setting the value of z to `999`:

```
self.addChild(@grass, z:999)
```

The layer that has a higher value of z will show up.

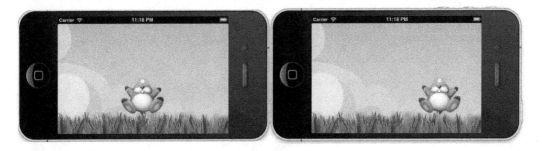

Adding touch events to the game

Now, let's add a touch event to the game:

1. Add the following code in the `game_layer.rb` file:

```
self.isTouchEnabled = true
```

2. Now add the following method to it:

```
def ccTouchesBegan(touches, withEvent:event)
  touch = touches.anyObject

  touch_location = self.convertTouchToNodeSpace(touch)
  @moles.each do |mole|
    if CGRectContainsPoint(mole.boundingBox, touch_location)
and !CGRectContainsPoint(@grass.boundingBox, touch_location)
      puts "You have clicked a mole"
    end
  end
end
```

In the first portion, we choose one of the touches we want to work with, get the location in the current view, and then call convertToGL to convert the coordinates to our current layout. This is important to do as we are in the landscape mode.

Next, come to the game logic. The CGRectContainsPoint(mole.boundingBox, touch_location) method will return true if someone clicks on the mole. But what if the user clicks on the mole behind the grass? For that, CGRectContainsPoint(@grass.boundingBox, touch_location) will return true if we have clicked on the grass. Therefore, CGRectContainsPoint(mole.boundingBox, touch_location) and !CGRectContainsPoint(@grass.boundingBox, touch_location) will only return true if we click on the mole at the right place. We will also print a message in the console to test the logic.

3. Let's run the application. When you click on the mole, you will get a message printed in the console:

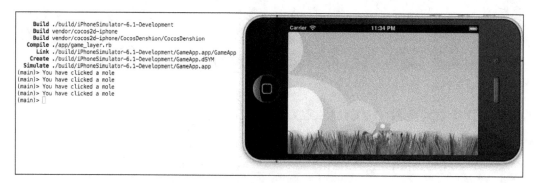

Adding scores

We need to give a purpose and sense of accomplishment to the user—that's one of the reasons why we play games. This can be done by calculating the score for the player every time there is a tap on the mole:

1. Add the following code to the `game_layer.rb` file:

   ```
   @score = 0
   @score_label = CCLabelTTF.labelWithString("Score: 0",
   fontName:"Verdana",fontSize: 14)
   @score_label.position = CGPointMake( 9*screen_size.width / 10,
   9*screen_size.height / 10)
   self.addChild(@score_label, z:999)
   ```

2. Then, update the `ccTouchesBegan` delegate in the `game_layer.rb` file:

   ```
   def ccTouchesBegan(touches, withEvent:event)
       touch = touches.anyObject

       touch_location = self.convertTouchToNodeSpace(touch)
       @moles.each do |mole|
         if CGRectContainsPoint(mole.boundingBox, touch_location)
   and !CGRectContainsPoint(@grass.boundingBox, touch_location)
           @score = @score + 10
           @score_label.setString("Score:"+ @score.to_s)
     end
       end
       end
   ```

3. Now run the application:

Games without any sounds are boring — let's add some sound

We're pretty close to having a workable game now. We just need to add some sound effects and music, and our game application will be complete. Playing sound in a game with Cocos2D is simple. We already have the `noise.wav` file in the `resource` folder; so let's use it on a few of our events:

Add the following code, which will play a sound when someone rightly clicks on the mole:

```
def ccTouchesBegan(touches, withEvent:event)
  touch = touches.anyObject

  touch_location = self.convertTouchToNodeSpace(touch)
  @moles.each do |mole|
    if CGRectContainsPoint(mole.boundingBox, touch_location) and
 !CGRectContainsPoint(@grass.boundingBox, touch_location)
      @score = @score + 10
      @score_label.setString("Score:"+ @score.to_s)
      SimpleAudioEngine.sharedEngine.playEffect "noise.wav"
    end
  end
end
```

Here we have finally completed a gaming application with RubyMotion. But don't submit this simple application to the App Store; use your imagination to make it an amazing application. Besides Cocos2D, there are many other gaming libraries that you can explore to create breathtaking apps. The following are a few that we recommend:

- iTGB for 2D Games: This is a 2D game engine
- Ston3D for iPhone: This is a 3D game engine
- SIO2Engine: This is a 3D game engine
- Unity3D Engine: This is a 3D game engine

Summary

This chapter was really exciting for us, and we hope you have learned a lot too. The following topics were covered:

- Understanding Cocos2D
- Creating a simple gaming application

So far we have learned all the major features of RubyMotion, and we even created a gaming application, but it is important to publish our application too. Next, we need to learn how to submit our valuable applications to Apple's App Store, so that they can be put in the hands of millions of iPhone and iPad users.

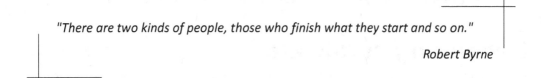

10
Getting Ready for the App Store

"There are two kinds of people, those who finish what they start and so on."

Robert Byrne

We have come a long way in learning RubyMotion to create iOS applications. Hopefully, we are now proficient in developing applications with RubyMotion. So far, we have gone from creating a simple iOS application to including the amazing device capabilities of iPhone and iPad with our RubyMotion project and then creating games. In the previous chapter, we learned how to write test cases and test our application automatically. We have now covered all the parts of a software life cycle, except our app is not in production yet. Apple has a specific way to share your finished app with the world. In this chapter, we will cover setting up your Mac to create your application bundle, to share it, and to distribute your application over the Apple App Store.

In this chapter, we will cover the following topics:

- Generating certificates
- Provisioning portals
- Setting up a RubyMotion project
- Testing on a device
- iTunes Connect
- Bundles for submission

Before you begin setting up your Mac for app distribution, you are required to enroll into the Apple Developer Program for iOS development (`https://developer.apple.com`). It is compulsory to enroll into this program, otherwise you will not be able to submit your application build to the App Store. Apple reviews each and every application before it is released to the App Store. You should also have a look at the Apple review guidelines, available at the iOS Dev Center, once you have your membership. These guidelines are important to understand for the smooth approval of your app; we will cover most of them as we proceed, but do go through them yourself too. These guidelines also contain **Human Interface Guidelines (HIG)**; many consider these guidelines as Apple's way of having a controlled environment for developers, but the prime purpose of these instructions is to create applications of a set standard and make them a class apart from other smartphones. So far, Apple has been successful in maintaining their good standard.

You should also set up your profile for your apps at `https://itunesconnect.apple.com/`; we will discuss more about this later in the chapter.

Generating certificates

To submit your application to the App Store, you require a developer certificate, a distribution certificate, a developer provisioning profile, and a distribution provisioning profile. In this section, we will bind your Mac with your iOS provisioning portal by generating certificates.

Once you log in to `https://developer.apple.com`, choose the iOS provisioning portal. Select the **Certificates** tab from the options provided in the left-hand side column as shown in the following screenshot:

If you are a first-time user, you need to first install the **Worldwide Developer Relations (WWDR)** intermediate certificate; this certificate binds your developer and distribution certificate to the Apple Certificate Authority. Download this and it will be installed in your keychain.

Next, let's create our developer certificate. To generate this, let's go back to our keychain application and navigate to **KeyChain Access Menu | Certificate Assistant | Request a certificate from certificate authority**.

Here, you have to use the same e-mail address with which you had registered for your developer account. We must add a unique name for this certificate and save it to the disk.

Now, let's go back to our developer account in our browser. Inside the **Development** tab, we have a **Request Certificate** option that shows all of the instructions that we have already completed and that are ready for our certificate.

Once uploaded, you will see **Pending Issuance**. Not a problem; refresh your browser, and your certificate will be uploaded. Download this and run; it will get stored in your keychain. Similarly, follow the same procedure for the distribution certificate.

Inside your keychain, in the certificate section you will see all of the installed certificates. Every certificate is a combination of two things: a certificate and a private key. It's good practice to make a copy of it and keep it in a safe place. In this way, if you change your machine, you will easily be able to download the certificate; but it will not work without the private key.

Do it yourself

Just like the developer profile for developing and testing in a development environment, we have a distribution profile that is used for distributing our application on the App Store.

Now that you know how to generate, upload, and install the Apple certificate on your Mac machine for your developer profile, why not try it yourself and distribute the profile. All you have to do is just follow these steps:

1. Generate the certificate using Certificate Assistant.
2. Upload it on the **Distribution certificate** tab.
3. Install it on your machine.

Provisioning profile

A provisioning profile binds numerous digital objects, such as our applications, certificates, and devices, together. A provisioning profile has two parts: one is our development provisioning profile and the other is the distribution profile.

App ID

Before we create a new provisioning profile, let's first create an app ID for our application. Inside the provisioning portal, we have a section for creating the app ID. It is necessary to create a new app ID for every application. This app ID is then used while generating a new provisioning profile.

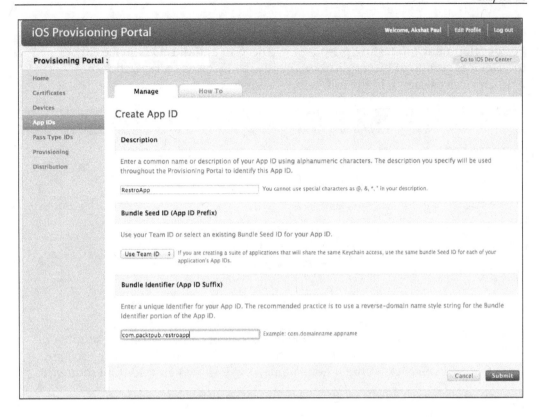

First, we add the description; this is how we will recognize our app ID in our provisioning portal. Next, we add a seed ID. (For first-time users, you will get an option to generate a new one.) Lastly, we add a bundle identifier. We are going to use this bundle identifier in the `Rakefile` of our RubyMotion project later on. The general nomenclature of naming a bundle identifier is the reverse domain notation, where **com** is followed by the domain name. In our case I have used **packtpub**, but you should add your domain name here. In the last part of the bundle identifier, add your application's name; in this case, we will use **Restroapp**.

> A bundle identifier is used to distinguish between various applications. We can use `com.domainname.*` for this purpose. An asterisk (*) symbol lets us use the same identifier for multiple apps. But we recommend naming your application for every identifier.

Adding devices

For development and testing purposes, we need to add our iOS devices in the **Devices** section of the application. Inside the **Devices** section, click on **Add Devices** as shown in the following screenshot:

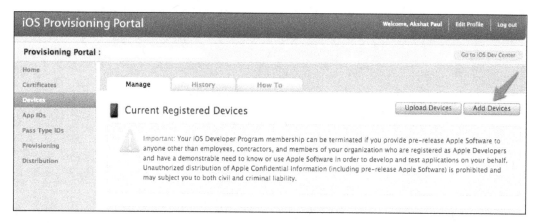

To test your application on your iPhone or iPad, simply add the UDID number of your device and a device name of your choice. The UDID number can be seen in iTunes. When you click on the iPhone name, it will show you a 40-digit sequence:

You must add all of the devices you want to test on, which we will be using during development. If the devices you want to test on are not present, the application won't be installed on that device.

> Apple allows you to add up to 100 iOS devices; this is strictly for development and testing purposes only.

Developer Provisioning Profile

Now that we have everything in place to create a new provisioning profile, let's do it by choosing the **Provisioning** option. The **Create new developer profile** form is divided into the following four sections:

- **Profile Name**: This is a label to recognize the profile.
- **Certificates**: Choose the developer certificate you have installed on your system. If it is a one-man workshop like mine, you will see only one option.
- **App ID**: Select the one we had created from the previous section for this application.
- **Devices**: These are the devices you want to test on.

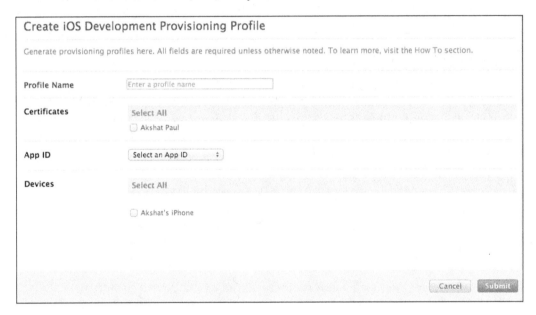

Once you submit this, you will see a pending status. Refresh your browser, and your provisioning profile will be ready. Download it and click on the file, and it will get installed in your Xcode. You can access all of the information related to this provisioning profile by navigating to **Xcode | Organiser | Provisioning Profiles | Devices**.

Do it yourself

Now that you know how to create a developer provisioning profile, why don't you try creating the distribution profile for yourself by performing the following steps:

1. Open the **Distribution** tab in the **Provisioning** section.

2. Create a new profile.

3. Download and install the profile.

Setting up the RubyMotion project

Next, let's set up our RubyMotion project; it will include the information we have collected previously.

Entitlements

Entitlements are used during the code-signing part of the build process. Many applications require access to device features; Apple requires you to specify the entitlements if you want to access a specific device feature. This can be added in the `Rakefile`. The entitlement method in the `Rakefile` lets you specify the appropriate keys and values in the following way:

```
Motion::Project::App.setup do |app|
  # ...
  app.entitlements['keychain-access-groups'] = [
    app.seed_id + '.' + app.identifier
  ]
end
```

In this example, if your application requires access to a keychain to store user credentials, you must send a request for `keychain-access-groups` by passing the application provisioning identifier and application identifier along with `seed_id` and the app identifier.

Info.plist settings

To provide the best experience to the users, iOS expects the presence of meta information in each application. This information is then used in various ways. Some of it is displayed to users and some may be used internally by the system to identify the application. These configuration settings are defined in Info.plist, which resides in the application's bundle.

In a RubyMotion project, the Info.plist file is defined in the Rakefile in a hash-like structure where you have a key-value pair. For example, we define CFBundleURLTypes in the following example:

```
Motion::Project::App.setup do |app|
  # ...
  app.info_plist['CFBundleURLTypes'] = [
    { 'CFBundleURLName' => 'com.packtpub.restroapp'}

  ]
end
```

The Rakefile does not cover all the possible settings, but it reveals the internal Info.plist data structure that one can modify, if at all needed. For more information and to check a list of other Info.plist properties, you can visit the Apple developer reference at http://developer.apple.com/library/ios/#documentation/General/Reference/InfoPlistKeyReference/Introduction/Introduction.html.

Building icons

Now that our machine is set up for the App Store, let's set up our RubyMotion project too. The first thing to do here is to set build icons. Since iOS devices, such as the iPhone, iPad, iPad mini, and retina displays come in a variety of screen sizes and display resolutions, Apple provides specific guidelines for creating icons to cater to each of them.

For our application icons, simply add these icons in the resources folder. They can have any random name, but it is a good idea to name them descriptively according to what they represent, such as icon_name-114 or icon-1024. Here, 114 and 1024 represent the size 114 x 114 for a standard app icon and 1024 x 1024 for an App Store icon, respectively.

Next, add the `icon` attribute in your `Rakefile` in the following way:

```
Motion::Project::App.setup do |app|
  # Use `rake config' to see complete project settings.
  app.name = 'Restaurant Application'
  app.icons  =  ['icon-114.png']
end
```

By default, these icons have a glossy effect on the upper half of the image, which is the traditional iPhone style. But you can change this by adding the following lines in your `Rakefile`:

```
Motion::Project::App.setup do |app|
  # Use `rake config' to see complete project settings.
  app.name = 'Restaurant Application'
  app.icons  =  ['icon-114.png']
  app.prerendered_icon = true
end
```

That's it. Our RubyMotion application is now ready with icons. Some tips for designing great icons are as follows:

- For best results, enlist the help of a professional graphic designer
- Use universal imagery that people will easily recognize
- Embrace simplicity
- The richer the icons are in texture, the better they are to look at
- Make the icons more detailed and more realistic
- Add detail and depth

As icons provide the first impression of your application, you must work extensively to ensure they look good. You can find more information related to icons and designs on the Apple developer reference at `http://developer.apple.com/library/ios/#documentation/userexperience/conceptual/mobilehig/IconsImages/IconsImages.html`.

Besides icons, we can have other resources, such as images and sound files. These can be included in the `resources` folder, and instances of these can be used throughout our application. For example, we can create the instance of the `hello.png` image with `UIImage.imageNamed("hello")`.

Configuring your application

Before we create the package that will be uploaded to the App Store review, we need to add some configuration settings so that Apple can recognize that the application is from a registered source. Here we will use the information from our provisioning profile, plus some general information related to our application.

All these settings, once again, go into our `Rakefile`. Some of the required settings that need to be fed are our iOS SDK version that we are using and our application version, such as 1.0, 1.3, and 2.0, which is always incremented for future releases. The deployment target is a minimal iOS version on which we want to run our application or anything that will work fine with our application. We also need to specify our identifier and provisioning profile details. This will be clear with the following example:

```
Motion::Project::App.setup do |app|
app.sdk_version = "6.0"
app.deployment_target = "5.0"
app.version = "1.0"
app.identifier = "com.packtpub.restroapp"
app.provisiong_profile = "/Users/your_name/Provisioning_Profiles/
random_sequence.mobileprovision"
end
```

 The provisioning profile details are different for development and distribution. Distribution profile details are used only when we want to submit or test apps on many devices.

Installing on a device

It's a good idea to test your application before you submit it to the App Store. Now that all our settings are in place, we just need to run the `rake device` command from the console. Before doing so, make sure your registered device in the provisioning portal is connected via USB to your Mac machine. The process may fail for any of the following reasons:

- The registered device is not connected to your machine via a USB
- An incorrect identifier or provisioning profile's details have been added
- The project uses an incorrect iOS version that is running on the device

iTunes Connect

Now we are done; but just before we create our application bundle and upload it, we need to set up our application on a separate portal (`https://itunesconnect.apple.com`). **iTunes Connect** has many options related to your application, such as **Sales and Trends**, **Catalog Reports**, **Developer Forums**, **Payments**, **Manage Your Application**, **Manage Users**, and many more. But, for now, we are just interested in the **Manage Your Application** option:

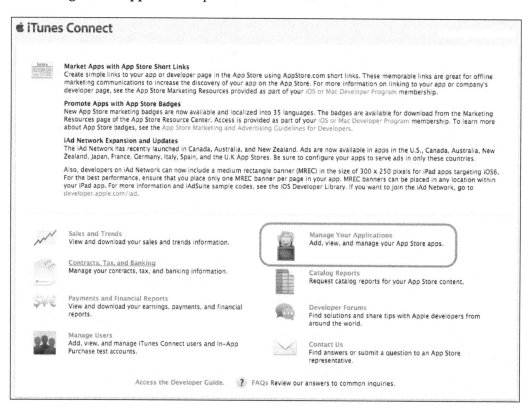

Once you have chosen **Manage Your Applications**, click on the button to add a new application to your catalog. This will show you the following form:

Enter the following information about your app.

Default Language	English	
App Name		
SKU Number		
Bundle ID	Select	

You can register a new Bundle ID here.

Enter your application's name in the **App Name** textbox. The SKU number is a desired, unique alphanumeric sequence that you have to enter. Select a **Bundle ID** option from the drop-down menu; since your iTunes Connect profile is coupled with your provisioning portal, you will get the right options in the dropdown automatically.

Once submitted, you will get the option of when to release the application, choosing the price tier (free or paid), and choosing which App Store will sell the application based on various countries. Following this window, another form will appear where you will have to fill in the description of your application, upload snapshots of various devices, add icons for the App Store, and fill in other logistic details, such as who to contact for support in case there are some issues related to the application.

Now that our application has been set up on iTunes Connect, we will next learn how to push our app for the App Store review.

Creating bundles for submission

The `rake archive` command generates a `.ipa` archive. This package is used for submitting our application to the App Store. The archive package can also be used for ad-hoc distribution to test the application on distributed devices.

Once we run the `rake archive` command, we will get the binary along with their appropriate distribution certificates. This is then uploaded on iTunes Connect with a special Apple utility named **Application Loader**.

With the Xcode installation, we automatically get the **Application Loaded** utility that we can access from our application's folder or access by simply making a spotlight search:

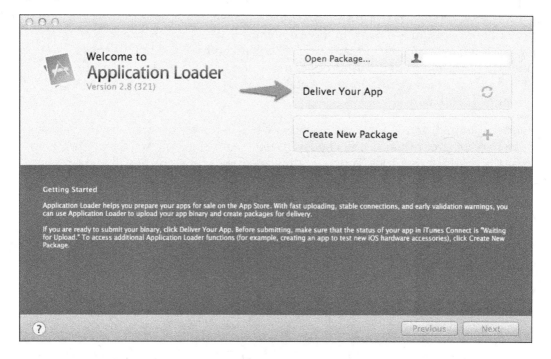

Choose the **Deliver Your App** option; this will indicate the name of the application iTunes Connect is waiting to upload. Choose your `.ipa` package from `./build/iPhoneOs_sdk_verson/Release/your_application.ipa`. Once this is done, you will see that the status of iTunes Connect has changed to **Received Binary**.

Great! Finally, we have submitted our application to the App Store. The Apple App Store takes a few days to review your application; you will see the status of your application change from **Waiting for Review** to **In Review** after a few days. In case there are any issues related to your application, the Apple team will first contact you using the details provided in iTunes Connect; and if the problem is not resolved, the application will get rejected. If this happens, you can resolve the issues faced by the review team and resubmit the app.

Summary

This chapter has covered the last step of an iOS application's life cycle. Let's recap what we have learned:

- How to generate certificates
- How to use the provisioning portal
- How to set up a RubyMotion project
- How to test on a device
- How to use iTunes Connect
- How to create bundles for submission

With this chapter, we have almost come to the end of our journey of learning how to use and craft iOS applications with RubyMotion. But this is just the tip of the iceberg. We still have to explore so many iOS SDK APIs to make the applications we have dreamt of. RubyMotion makes even this part stress-free with the use of gems. In the final chapter, we will learn how to use some of the most popular RubyMotion gems, and how to contribute back to the RubyMotion community by creating our own gems.

11
Extending RubyMotion

The DRY principle states the following:

> *"Every piece of knowledge must have a single, unambiguous, authoritative representation within a system."*

We are now approaching the end of this book. So far we have learned how to quickly make iOS applications with RubyMotion. To make this process even more rapid, RubyMotion lets us use special RubyMotion-flavored gems and wrappers. **Gems** and **wrappers** are Ruby programs that are wrapped into a self-contained format. These are generally open source projects, which other developers can use in their applications or can even contribute back to these projects. Fortunately, RubyMotion has a very enthusiastic community; within months of launching RubyMotion's tool chain, plenty of gems were introduced that implement many laborious tasks fairly quickly. In this chapter, we will learn how to augment our application by using RubyMotion-flavored gems. The following topics will be covered in this chapter:

- RubyMotion gems
- CocoaPods

RubyMotion gems

Use of gems is based on the programming practice of **Don't Repeat Yourself** (DRY), which states that when some piece of code is ready to use and is available, why bother working on it again. The RubyMotion community may be very young right now, but it already has some amazing gems that make a lot of tiring tasks pretty easy. Some gems even target challenging functionalities in a very simple manner.

In this chapter we will cover the following RubyMotion-flavored gems:

- Teacup
- BubbleWrap
- `motion-addressbook`

Teacup – say goodbye to Xcode and XIB files!

Designing a UI for iOS apps is a tough job, especially for developers who have worked previously on easy-to-learn-and-implement web technologies. **Teacup** is a gem that will make your life really easy. Teacup augments your ability to quickly design and style the views of your RubyMotion application; you can easily create layouts while keeping your code DRY.

Let's create an application and learn how easy it is to use Teacup:

```
$motion create TeaCupMotion
```

We will be using **Bundler** (which is also a Ruby gem) to install all our gems. Bundler also helps us manage application dependencies, so that the exact version of the gems used are available for the application to run.

 Bundler comes as a default dependency manager for popular frameworks such as Ruby on Rails.

Let's add Bundler to our application:

1. Update the `Rakefile` with the following lines of code:
   ```
   $:.unshift("/Library/RubyMotion/lib")
   require 'motion/project'
   require 'bundler'
   Bundler.require
   ```

2. With Bundler, we require a Gemfile in which we can mention details about the gems we will use with our application. Next, let's create a Gemfile and add the following lines of code in it:

```
source "https://rubygems.org"

gem "teacup"
```

So, in the future, if you want to add any new gem to your project, you can simply add it to this file.

3. Next, let's run `bundle install` and we're good to go:

```
bundle install
```

 The `bundle install` command adds a `Gemfile.lock` file to your repository. This ensures that other developers on your app, as well as your deployment environment, will all use the same third-party code that you are using now.

4. Next, update the `app_delegate.rb` file with the following code:

```
class AppDelegate
  def application(application, didFinishLaunchingWithOptions:launc
hOptions)
    @window = UIWindow.alloc.initWithFrame(UIScreen.mainScreen.
bounds)
    myNavController = RootController.alloc.init

    @window.rootViewController = UINavigationController.alloc.init
WithRootViewController(myNavController)
    @window.rootViewController.wantsFullScreenLayout = true
    @window.makeKeyAndVisible
    true
  end
end
```

In this code, we are only initializing an instance of `RootController`, just like we do with every application. As you may remember, the controller is where all our application logic resides.

So far, in various chapters we have made RubyMotion iOS applications in a traditional way. Let's use Teacup in our application this time, and add styles by making use of its Cascading Style Sheets (CSS) type syntax.

Let's create a directory named `style` and add a new file with the name of `style.rb` in it. Add the following code to the `style.rb` file in the `style` folder:

```
Teacup::Stylesheet.new(:style) do

  style :your_layout,
    landscape: true

  style UILabel,
    textColor: UIColor.blueColor
  style :label,
    text: 'Awesome',
    backgroundColor: UIColor.whiteColor,
    top: 10,
    left: 100,
    width: 100,
    height: 20

end
```

Let's understand the preceding code:

1. First, we have created a stylesheet named `style`.

   ```
   Teacup::Stylesheet.new(:style) do
   ...
   end
   ```

   This convention is provided by Teacup to create a new stylesheet.

2. Next, we have created a specific layout for your views, using CSS-based syntax.

   ```
   style :your_layout,
     landscape: true
   ```

   This will create a style named `your_layout` and will enable the landscape rotation (otherwise, only portrait orientation is enabled).

3. Next, we have added style for all `UILabel` instances.

```
style UILabel,
    textColor: UIColor.blueColor
```

The preceding line of code gives text color to all `UILabel` instances that are defined inside the style. Since we apply a style to all the labels when using `UILabel`, if we want to style a specific element, we have to add the following commands:

```
style :label,
    text: 'Awesome',
    backgroundColor: UIColor.whiteColor,
    top: 10,
    left: 100,
    width: 100,
    height: 20
```

Here, `label` is like a class. This will do the styling for the label.

To understand this better, let's create a view. Perform the following steps to create a view:

1. Create a file named `root_view_controller.rb` and add the following code to it:

```
class RootController < UIViewController

    stylesheet :style

    layout :your_layout do
        @label1 = subview(UILabel, :label)

    end

    def shouldAutorotateToInterfaceOrientation(orientation)
        autorotateToOrientation(orientation)
    end

end
```

As we have created a new controller file, we must make the corresponding changes to the `app_delegate.rb` file. Make these changes in your `app_delegate.rb` file as shown in the previous chapters.

In the preceding code snippet, first we have given the stylesheet a name, which is done using `stylesheet:style`, and then we have specified a layout named `your_layout` and passed `label` : `@label1 = subview(UILabel, :label)` to it.

2. Let's fire up the terminal and test our application.

    `$rake`

    The following is the output:

We can see the text **Awesome** appear on the simulator screen and it is styled as we have defined in the stylesheet.

 Teacup implements the `viewDidLoad` method and instantiates any views. If you want to implement your own `viewDidLoad` method, make sure to call super.

We can also define different stylesheets for changing dimensions as we rotate the device, such as the landscape and portrait modes. Let's try this in our next example.

3. Now update the stylesheet, that is, the `style.rb` file, with the following code:

```
style :label,
text: 'Awesome',
backgroundColor: UIColor.whiteColor,
top: 10,
left: 100,
width: 100,
height: 20,
landscape: {
    backgroundColor: UIColor.redColor,
}
```

4. Run the application and rotate the screen from the simulator menu by navigating to **Hardware | Rotate Left**. You will see that as the screen rotates the background color of the label changes.

5. Now, let's do a few more things in the same example. Add the following code in the `style.rb` file:

```
style UITextField,                      # Defining styles based on
view
class instead
  textColor: UIColor.redColor

  style :field,
  left:   10,
  top:    10,
  width:  200,
  height: 30,
  landscape: {
    width: 360  # make it wide in landscape view
  }

  style :search, extends: :field,
  backgroundColor: UIColor.whiteColor,
  left: 20,
```

```
top: 70,
placeholder: 'Search Box'
style :search_new, extends: :field,
backgroundColor: UIColor.redColor,
left: 20,
top: 110,
placeholder: 'Search Box'
```

Here we have created two text field boxes.

6. Now, update the `root_controller.rb` file.

```
layout :your_layout do
  @label1 = subview(UILabel, :label)
  @search = subview(UITextField, :search)
  @one_more_search = subview(UITextField, :search_new)

end
```

7. Let's test our application in the simulator.

$rake

The following is the output:

With the preceding example, we can see how easy it is to design views with the Teacup gem; it has delivered a way to create interfaces programmatically with ease. We have shared a few of the features of this amazing gem; you can explore more at `https://github.com/rubymotion/teacup`.

BubbleWrap – making Cocoa APIs more Ruby-like

BubbleWrap is a collection of very well-tested helpers and wrappers used to wrap Cocoa SDK code and provide more Ruby-like APIs for RubyMotion. It provides wrappers for a lot of iOS Cocoa SDK code, such as camera, notification center, HTTP, and many more.

We can do a lot of things very easily. For example, to perform a GET HTTP request with BubbleWrap, we require the following simple code snippet:

```
BW::HTTP.get("https://twitter.com/rubymotion") do |response|
  p response.body.to_str
end
```

In *Chapter 6*, *Device Capability – Power Unleashed*, we have learned about device capabilities—implementing camera functionalities in your app. We have written quite a lot of code there, but with BubbleWrap things get really simplified. We only require the following code snippet for using a camera in our application:

```
BW::Device.camera.front.picture(media_types: [:movie, :image]) do
|result|
  image_view = UIImageView.alloc.initWithImage(result[:original_
image])
end
```

BubbleWrap also provides a module named App that can be used while running the application. To understand this, perform the following steps:

1. First, create a small sample application.

    $motion create UseBubbleWrap

2. Update the Rakefile to include a Bundler that will help us install the BubbleWrap gem easily.

    ```
    require 'bundler'
    Bundler.require
    ```

3. As shown in the last section, let's add a `Gemfile` to our project with the following code:

```
source :rubygems
gem 'bubble-wrap'
```

4. Run the following command to install the BubbleWrap gem:

```
$bundle install
```

5. Next, let's fire up the terminal to test the `App` module on the console:

```
$rake
```

6. To use the `App` module, run the following commands in REPL:

```
(main) > App.name
=> "UseBubbleWrap"
```

```
(main) > App.identifier
=> "com.yourcompany.UseBubbleWrap"
```

```
(main) > App.documents_path
=> "/Users/abhishek/Library/Application Support/iPhone
Simulator/6.1/Applications/3CF89A96-F390-4A7D-89B8-2F0E7B54A38A/
Documents"
```

```
(main) > App.resources_path
=> "/Users/abhishek/Library/Application Support/iPhone
Simulator/6.1/Applications/3CF89A96-F390-4A7D-89B8-2F0E7B54A38A/
UseBubbleWrap.app"
```

```
(main) > App.frame
=> #<CGRect origin=#<CGPoint x=0.0 y=20.0> size=#<CGSize
width=320.0 height=460.0>>
(main) > App.states
=> {}
```

```
(main) > App.shared
=> #<UIApplication:0x9530920>
```

```
(main) > App.current_locale
=> #<__NSCFLocale:0x966a040>
```

```
(main)> App.alert("This is nice!!")
=> #<UIAlertView:0xa8433f0>


(main)>  App.run_after(0.5) {  p "It's #{Time.now}"    }
=> #<__NSCFTimer:0x93760c0>
(main)> "It's 2013-05-10 18:47:34 +0530"
```

7. There is another module named `Device` that provides many options related to the current device. Let's once again fire up REPL in our terminal and execute the following commands:

```
$rake
(main)> Device.iphone?
=> true

(main)> Device.ipad?
=> false

(main)> Device.front_camera?
"This method (front_camera?) is DEPRECATED. Transition to using
Device.camera.front?"
=> false

(main)>  Device.screen.width
=> 320.0

(main)> Device.screen.height
=> 480.0

(main)> Device.orientation
=> :portrait
```

There are tons of helpers that come with the BubbleWrap gem. It will be helpful for your project if you have a look at the BubbleWrap documentation at http://bubblewrap.io/.

motion-addressbook – access phonebook easily

In *Chapter 6, Device Capability – Power Unleashed*, we had discussed in detail how to use the Address Book technology for iOS devices. In this section, we will use a special gem for RubyMotion named `motion-addressbook` that simplifies using the Address Book.

We will perform the following actions in this section:

- Create a sample app with the `motion-addressbook` gem
- Pull the data from the device's Address Book
- Display it on the screen

Let's start by performing the following steps:

1. Create a sample application.

   $motion create AddressBook_example

2. Next, let's include the `motion-addressbook` gem in the `Gemfile`.

   ```
   source :rubygems
   gem 'bubble-wrap'
   gem 'motion-addressbook'
   ```

3. Bundle install from the command line to include this gem in our project:

   $bundle install

4. Let's create a file named `addressbook_controller.rb` in which we will add a button and three labels. With the button, we will access our address book and choose the desired contact. In the labels, we will display the data of the user, which we have copied from the address book. Add the following code in your `addressbook_controller.rb` file:

   ```
   def viewDidLoad
       view.backgroundColor = UIColor.underPageBackgroundColor
       load_button
       load_labels
   end

   def load_button

       @phonebook_button = UIButton.buttonWithType(UIButtonTypeRoundedRect)
       @phonebook_button.frame = [[50, 20], [200, 50]]
   ```

```
    @phonebook_button.setTitle("Click from Contacts",
forState:UIControlStateNormal)
    @phonebook_button.addTarget(self, action: :addressbook_access,
forControlEvents:UIControlEventTouchUpInside)
    view.addSubview(@phonebook_button)

  end


  def load_labels

    @first_name = UILabel.new
    @first_name.text = 'First Name'
    @first_name.frame = [[100,100],[150,50]]

    @last_name = UILabel.new
    @last_name.text = 'Last Name'
    @last_name.frame = [[100,160],[150,50]]

    @organization = UILabel.new
    @organization.text = 'Organization'
    @organization.frame = [[100,220],[150,50]]

    view.addSubview(@first_name)
    view.addSubview(@last_name)
    view.addSubview(@organization)
  end
```

5. Add the following code in the `app_delegate.rb` file so that our delegate points to our address book controller:

```
class AppDelegate
  def application(application, didFinishLaunchingWithOptions:launc
hOptions)

  @window = UIWindow.alloc.initWithFrame(UIScreen.mainScreen.
bounds)
    @window.rootViewController = AddressbookController.alloc.init
    @window.makeKeyAndVisible


    true
  end
end
```

6. Let's fire up the terminal and run our app in a simulator to check if we are able to see our three labels and a button.

    $rake

    The following is the output:

7. In the preceding code snippet, we have mentioned a method named `addressbook_access`. To access the Address Book, we need to use the `AddressBook` picker that lets us open the device's Address Book in our application and pick data from it. With this method, we will be doing the same. Let's create this method in our `addressbook_controller.rb` file and add the following code to it:

    ```
    def addressbook_access

      AddressBook.pick { |person|
        if person
          first_name = person.attributes[:first_name]
          last_name = person.attributes[:last_name]
          org = person.attributes[:organization]
          @first_name.text = first_name
    ```

```
        @last_name.text = last_name
        @organization.text = org

    else
      # write some cancel code
    end
  }

  end
```

8. Let's fire up the terminal and run our app in a simulator to check if we are able to access the Address Book and import the desired contact details in our application.

   $rake

   The following is the output:

9. Once we select any contact, we will get its details on our application, as shown in the following screenshot:

That's it, we are done. It's the same application we had created in *Chapter 6, Device Capability – Power Unleashed*, but with motion-addressbook, we have substantially less code.

Let's understand what we have done here. The motion-addressbook gem gives us many options to easily use the device's Address Book. In the addressbook_access method, we have used the AddressBook picker by using AddressBook.pick, which opens up the device's Address Book for us. Once we select any contact, we get a person object that has a hash of all the attributes of the selected contact.

In our example, we have used the first_name, last_name, and organization values from the selected person object. However, the motion-addressbook gem has many more options that make working with the Address Book framework faster and easier. A few of them are as follows:

- To create a new contact.

```
AddressBook::Person.new
#<AddressBook::Person:0xc360bc0 @address_book=nil @ab_person=nil @
attributes={}>
```

- To pull all the records from the address book.

```
AddressBook::Person.all
[#<AddressBook::Person:0x9d78c80 @address_book=#<__
NSCFType:0xc0db6d0> @ab_person=#<__NSCFType:0x9d77ea0> @
attributes={:first_name=>"Abhishek", :last_name=>"Nalwaya",
:organization=>"Fun Inc."}>, #<AddressBook::Person:0x78f0a20
@address_book=#<__NSCFType:0xc0db6d0> @ab_person=#<__
NSCFType:0x9d78520> @attributes={:first_name=>"Akshat",
:last_name=>"Paul", :organization=>"PacktPub"}>,
#<AddressBook::Person:0x78a5eb0 @address_book=#<__
NSCFType:0xc0db6d0> @ab_person=#<__NSCFType:0x9d788b0> @
attributes={:first_name=>"Laurent", :last_name=>"Sansonetti",
:organization=>"HipByte"}>, #<AddressBook::Person:0x78c06e0
@address_book=#<__NSCFType:0xc0db6d0> @ab_person=#<__
NSCFType:0x9d78700> @attributes={:first_name=>"Manu", :last_
name=>"Singhal", :organization=>"Ruby Inc"}>]
```

- To get a list of records based on a specific attribute.

```
AddressBook::Person.find_all_by_organization('HipByte')
```

- To get a list of records based on many conditions.

```
AddressBook::Person.where(:email => 'akshatpaul@abc.com',
:organization => 'Fun Inc')
```

- To create a new contact.

```
AddressBook::Person.create(:first_name => 'Shi', :last_name =>
'Foo', :email => shi@foo.com')
```

CocoaPods – managing Objective-C libraries

CocoaPods is the best way to manage library dependencies in Objective-C projects. CocoaPods was originally designed to be integrated in Objective-C Xcode projects, but it can readily be used in RubyMotion projects using the `motion-cocoapods` gem.

Installing CocoaPods with RubyMotion

Perform the following steps to install CocoaPods with RubyMotion:

1. Install CocoaPods.

    ```
    $sudo gem install cocoapods
    ```

2. Set up CocoaPods.

    ```
    $pod setup
    ```

3. Install motion-cocoapods to work with RubyMotion.

    ```
    $sudo gem install motion-cocoapods
    ```

Now we are all set to use CocoaPods in our RubyMotion project. Add the following code in the Rakefile:

```
Motion::Project::App.setup do |app|
  app.pods do
    dependency 'Reachability'
  end
end
```

So, next time when you build your code, it will automatically download the library for you. Then you can use the Objective-C CocoaPods in your project.

For detailed documentation on CocoaPods, visit http://cocoapods.org/.

Summary

In this chapter, we have learned the following topics:

*   RubyMotion Gems

    *   Teacup: A community-driven DSL for creating user interfaces on iOS.

    *   BubbleWrap: A collection of (tested) helpers and wrappers used to wrap CocoaTouch code and provide more Ruby-like APIs.

    *   motion-addressbook: A gem to perform different actions on the iOS Address Book.

*   CocoaPods: It is the best way to manage library dependencies in Objective-C and RubyMotion projects

What next?

Congratulations, we have covered a lot in the last 11 chapters and we are sure you now know a lot more about RubyMotion than you did at the outset.

We have learned a lot of things during this journey—beginning with installing RubyMotion, understanding the RubyMotion folder structure, debugging our application, introducing RubyMotion objects, creating an MVC application, playing with the user interface, using device capabilities such as the camera, gestures, persistence storage, writing test cases, creating games, using RubyMotion-flavored gems, and submitting the application to App Store. That's a lot of stuff!

So, what can be done next from here? The answer to this question is *plenty of things!* There is still a lot to discover in RubyMotion and the iOS SDK; so from here, the first thing we can do is grab a book that explores the iOS SDK in detail. The best source for anything related to iOS SDK is Apple's Developer Reference at `https://developer.apple.com/`. All things at Apple's Developer Reference are in Objective-C, but now we have the skills to translate verbose Objective-C code to learn and clean RubyMotion code.

Next, keep yourself updated with the latest happenings in the RubyMotion ecosystem with the RubyMotion blog (`http://blog.rubymotion.com`) and Developer Center (`http://www.rubymotion.com/developer-center/`). The RubyMotion blog keeps us updated with the RubyMotion world—what's new in this version or what's in store for the future of RubyMotion. Developer Center is a great source for API references, some quick tutorials, and the latest articles on technology. For RubyMotion wrappers and libraries, you can visit `http://rubymotion-wrappers.com/`. This web page is a one-stop shop for details on available wrappers and is updated often.

To discuss any issue, you must join the RubyMotion community at its Google group (`https://groups.google.com/forum/?fromgroups#!forum/rubymotion`). This group is a great place to interact with the vibrant RubyMotion community.

Finally, create apps! There is no better way to master a technology than learning on your own in a real-world scenario. You can contribute to the community by creating wrappers and gems—that's a great way to acquire expertise on a specific area of a technology. We hope you have enjoyed reading and learning with this book, and have now evolved as an iOS RubyMotion developer; we are very excited about RubyMotion, just like you, and look forward to seeing your work making a mark in the iOS and RubyMotion world.

Index

**Thank you for buying
RubyMotion iOS Develoment
Essentials**

About Packt Publishing

Packt, pronounced 'packed', published its first book "*Mastering phpMyAdmin for Effective MySQL Management*" in April 2004 and subsequently continued to specialize in publishing highly focused books on specific technologies and solutions.

Our books and publications share the experiences of your fellow IT professionals in adapting and customizing today's systems, applications, and frameworks. Our solution based books give you the knowledge and power to customize the software and technologies you're using to get the job done. Packt books are more specific and less general than the IT books you have seen in the past. Our unique business model allows us to bring you more focused information, giving you more of what you need to know, and less of what you don't.

Packt is a modern, yet unique publishing company, which focuses on producing quality, cutting-edge books for communities of developers, administrators, and newbies alike. For more information, please visit our website: www.packtpub.com.

Writing for Packt

We welcome all inquiries from people who are interested in authoring. Book proposals should be sent to author@packtpub.com. If your book idea is still at an early stage and you would like to discuss it first before writing a formal book proposal, contact us; one of our commissioning editors will get in touch with you.

We're not just looking for published authors; if you have strong technical skills but no writing experience, our experienced editors can help you develop a writing career, or simply get some additional reward for your expertise.

Xcode 4 iOS Development Beginner's Guide

ISBN: 978-1-84969-130-7   Paperback: 432 pages

Use the powerful Xcode 4 suite of tools to build applications for the iPhone and iPad from scratch

1. Learn how to use Xcode 4 to build simple, yet powerful applications with ease

2. Each chapter builds on what you have learned already

3. Learn to add audio and video playback to your applications

PhoneGap 2.x Mobile Application Development Hotshot

ISBN: 978-1-84951-940-3   Paperback: 388 pages

Create exciting apps for mobile devices using PhoneGap

1. Ten apps included to help you get started on your very own exciting mobile app

2. These apps include working with localization, social networks, geolocation, as well as the camera, audio, video, plugins, and more

3. Apps cover the spectrum from productivity apps, educational apps, all the way to entertainment and games

4. Explore design patterns common in apps designed for mobile devices

Please check **www.PacktPub.com** for information on our titles

Ruby and MongoDB Web Development Beginner's Guide

ISBN: 978-1-84951-502-3   Paperback: 332 pages

Create dynamic web applications by combining the power of Ruby and MongoDB

1. Step-by-step instructions and practical examples to creating web applications with Ruby and MongoDB

2. Learn to design the object model in a NoSQL way

3. Create objects in Ruby and map them to MongoDB

Xcode 4 Cookbook

ISBN: 978-1-84969-334-9   Paperback: 402 pages

Over 100 recipes to build your own fun and exciting iOS applications

1. Learn how to go about developing some simple, yet powerful applications with ease using recipes and example code

2. Teaches how to use the features of iOS 6 to integrate Facebook, Twitter, iCloud, and Airplay into your applications

3. Lots of step-by-step recipe examples with ample screenshots right through to application deployment to the Apple App Store to get you up to speed in no time, with helpful hints along the way

Please check **www.PacktPub.com** for information on our titles